BEHOLD
I Do a New Thing

TRANSFORMING COMMUNITIES
OF FAITH

C. Kirk Hadaway

THE
PILGRIM
PRESS

Cleveland

This book is dedicated

to my children,

Chelsea and Colin

The Pilgrim Press, 700 Prospect Avenue, Cleveland, Ohio 44115-1100 U.S.A.
pilgrimpress.com
© 2001 by C. Kirk Hadaway
All rights reserved. Published 2001

Grateful acknowledgement for permission to reprint from Marc Gellman, *Does God Have a Big Toe? Stories about Stories in the Bible.* Copyright © 1989 Marc Gellman. Used by permission of HarperCollins Publishers.

Printed in the United States of America on acid-free paper

06 05   5 4 3

Library of Congress Cataloging-in-Publication Data
Hadaway, C. Kirk.
    Behold I do a new thing : transforming communities of faith / C. Kirk Hadaway.
       p.   cm.
    Includes bibliographical references.
    ISBN 0-8298-1430-2 (pbk. : alk. paper)
    1. Church renewal.   I. Title.

BV600.3 .H33   2001
263—dc21

                                                                    2001032860

Contents

Figures

A HELPFUL THORN?

THIS BOOK IS A SEQUEL of sorts to a previous book, *Rerouting the Protestant Mainstream*, which I wrote with David Roozen in 1995. That book led to many opportunities to talk with local church pastors and other church leaders about revitalizing churches and denominational structures. My first speaking engagement was with the national staff of the Unitarian Universalist Association at their offices in Boston, Massachusetts. A second presentation was made to the national leadership of the Southern Baptist Convention at their missionary training center outside Richmond, Virginia. My third engagement was a one-day retreat with the pastors and staff of the Penn Northeast Conference of the United Church of Christ at a local church in Wilkes Barre, Pennsylvania. These events led to an evolving series of presentations that used *Rerouting the Protestant Mainstream* as a foundation. To this base, I added material from my reading, my experiences in churches, congregational research, interviews with parish ministers, and the comments of laity and ministers who attended my workshops, retreats, and lectures. Each event was an interactive process, and I learned much from those who attended these workshops and seminars—even from those who strenuously disagreed with me. Indeed, I probably learned the most from people who stood up and said things like, "I agree with most of what you said, but I really have a problem with. . . ."

In 1996 I wrote the first chapter of this book prior to a three-month sabbatical from my work at the United Church Board for Homeland Ministries (UCBHM). The muses stayed away during the sabbatical itself, however, and I wrote only one more chapter during that period, which I later threw away. In the fall of 1998 I was granted a leave of absence from UCBHM and completed the bulk of this book during a month of furious work and limited social contact. Rather than having a single chapter that made me feel guilty about not finishing the book, now I almost had a manuscript. Still, it took many more months to write the final chapters, and then re-edit an ever-evolving manuscript. Unfortunately, more reading, speaking, research, and talking with others about the subject of congregational vitality led to the need to rewrite four of the chapters that I had thought were finished. Now I understand why it takes people five years or more to write a book. In truth, this is a book that I could continue to write for the rest of my life. It has evolved over the past five years and would evolve further if it were not the time to say, "it is finished."

The book is about the same thing as *Rerouting the Protestant Mainstream* was about—congregational revitalization or renewal. It is not about church growth or decline. It does not address the issue of how to turn around membership decline, at least not directly. But one of the reasons I have written it is my concern about the loss of membership that has sapped the strength of mainline Protestant denominations in North America. Vital churches that are clear about their reason for being tend to be growing churches, but growth doesn't lead to vitality. It's the other way around.

This is not a practical, how-to-do-it book. Nor is it a book of tips or resources. *Rerouting the Protestant Mainstream* was criticized for not being those things, and this book is even less useful as a guide or handbook. Instead, it attempts to flesh out a process by which churches might actualize what the earlier book only imagined. This book encourages the reader to begin a journey that will create the capacity for renewal and revitalization. But it does not give specific directions or provide a map. Each journey is unique. It is not a matter of "half the fun is in the getting there." *All* of the fun is in the getting there, because there is no *there* to be gotten to. The goal, if it can be called a goal, is to engage a process of continuous incarnation, flowering and fruiting, that cannot be predicted nor controlled. It can only be cultivated, planted and pruned, nurtured and nourished.

There is very little "telling what to do" in this book. If I thought I knew what your church ought to do, and if I thought it would help, I would do the telling. Yet I know that there is no single answer to our problems and telling what should be done is useless anyway. It doesn't work with teenage children. It doesn't work with your parishioners. And it doesn't work with you or me. All lasting change in organisms and organizations results from systemic processes, not from single causes. This book is about engaging a fluid cycle of change and augmenting that flow in positive directions. The results of the process may be what we wanted in the first place, but if we were to pursue desired results directly, they would elude us. Thus we worry about the process rather than the specific outcome. We can never predict specific outcomes anyway, but if the cycle is generative and incarnational, good things will result. We trust in God, not in our preconceived notions about the way things ought to be.

In this book you will read some things that may seem rather critical and extreme. I don't want to be harsh, but I *do* want to offend you. I hope you do not find this book particularly enjoyable or agreeable. Indeed, I hope you will disagree with me frequently. It is not my purpose to reinforce opinions that you already have. I also do not believe that I am right and you are wrong. My purpose is not to lead you to accept my opinions. My purpose is to refocus awareness, so you will see your opinions, my opinions, and the opinions of others in a different light.

I want to provoke you to look at things from a different perspective—to step outside your usual pattern of thinking about the church. Doing so requires a little shock now and then. That is why some of what I say may seem to be overly critical, cynical, or exaggerated. I don't intend to offend, but a little offense may be necessary.

Anthony de Mello refers to the approach I am taking in this book with the rhetorical question: "A thorn can be dislodged by means of another thorn, can't it?"[1] It is my hope you find this book provocative (even painful) and, above all, useful in digging out a few thorns. Everything—including the new model introduced in chapters 4 and 5—was written with this purpose in mind.

There is no fully formed vision of a perfect church in this book. There is no silver bullet. There is no single answer, nor even a "faithful fix." But I hope reading this book will help you see that your church can provide a better, and more realistic, taste of God's Realm. Whatever you do will be based on what you are now, using the ingredients that you have on hand. You will help create or "bake" something new, wonderful, and unique to your situation.

This book is very personal. I use many examples from my own experience, frequently from outside the church context. I would have preferred a less personal approach, but this was the only way I could find to project a realistic sense of what I was talking about. It is not an exercise in narcissism, or at least I hope not.

---

1. Anthony de Mello, *More One Minute Nonsense* (Chicago: Loyola University Press, 1993), 1. When we use a thorn to dig out another thorn, the thorn we use may hurt, but it does not remain in the skin to fester. Thus, I am not asking the reader to replace one belief about the church with another.

I would like to think the principles considered here are applicable to all churches. It would have been foolish, however, to write a book that was so general that all churches would find it equally useful. Furthermore, the book deals with a series of problems. The problems that I chose to consider are those that are particularly acute among predominantly white Protestant churches in Canada and the United States. I deal with both mainline and evangelical churches, but the solution structures presented here probably will not be palatable to many theologically conservative churches. But this is not a "liberal" book. It challenges assumptions in all directions and includes something to offend everyone. As Anthony de Mello says, you have to dance your dance and this is my own step. I hope you find it interesting, provocative, and useful. If you don't, I still hope that it helps you look at churches in a slightly different way.

The title for this book is taken from Isaiah 43:19: "Behold I do a new thing, now it shall spring forth . . ." (DARBY). The context is that of redemption and renewal and the subject is that of new life in surprising places. I hope that it captures my sense of anticipated vitality for mainline churches.

I have many people to thank. Several individuals read previous versions of the manuscript and provided needed advice and encouragement. I particularly thank Bill Green, Larry Peers, Tina Brochu, and Nurya Lindburg for their helpful comments and enthusiasm during the early stages of my writing.

Because I don't preach—at least in the form of pulpit-delivered sermons—I needed a lot of help with the chapter on preaching, "Words for Liberation." Here I turned to Robert Marrone, pastor of St. Peter Church in Cleveland, Ohio, and F. Morgan Roberts, retired pastor of Shadyside Presbyterian Church in Pittsburgh, Pennsylvania (and interim pastor at Independent Presbyterian Church, Birmingham, Alabama, and at First Presbyterian Church, Lexington, Kentucky). As people say in the South, they can preach! They also have something to say which frequently "gets under your skin." I thank them for their patience in answering my endless questions about worship, sermons, and what they are trying to communicate. If you ever have the chance to attend worship where they are preaching, you owe it to yourself to go. As the chapter was being rewritten in the spring of 2000, Sarah Lammert, pastor of the Unitarian Universalist Church of Ogden, Utah, provided many helpful comments and correctives.

I also thank Penny Long Marler for her advice and ideas that I have solicited and borrowed over the years. From our conversations and her sermons,

I have learned much about the art of communication and the need for a fresh perspective on unexamined assumptions.

I thank Thomas Dipko, Rip Noble, and the United Church Board for Homeland Ministries for the opportunity to lead workshops and seminars in various settings of the United Church of Christ and with our ecumenical partners. This really wasn't in my job description, but they let me do it, and I am grateful for the freedom that they allowed.

Finally, I thank John Thomas, General Minister and President of the United Church of Christ, for his interest and encouragement, Diane Strickland for her insightful comments about the nearly completed manuscript, and my editors at The Pilgrim Press, Kim M. Sadler and Timothy G. Staveteig, for their willingness to put their imprint on this effort to help the local church.

Behold I Do a New Thing

Chapter one

TO CHANGE OR STAY THE SAME

AT A CONSULTATION A FEW YEARS AGO for a regional judicatory, a local church pastor listened patiently to my presentation from *Rerouting the Protestant Mainstream* and its prescription for mainline renewal.[1] During the question and answer session, he said: "I pastor a declining church in a small town in the hills of Eastern Pennsylvania. Our membership is getting older, and even though our services are no longer held in German, most of our members have German backgrounds, and we can't seem to attract anyone new. How can our church hold onto its German heritage and still give something meaningful to people who don't share it?"

I don't remember exactly what I said in response, but I do remember how uneasy I felt as he described his church. My first thought was, "well . . . you ain't got much hope." But I didn't have to tell him that his situation was grim. He already knew it. What he wanted to know was how a church like his—a declining ethnic congregation with identity problems—could change in a direction that would give it a new lease on life.

Church leaders (and church consultants) often "write off" older, plateaued, or declining churches in order to focus on newer, more healthy congregations for which change comes more easily. Pursuing such a strategy may be shortsighted, however, because the majority of churches in North America are stable or declining—including most conservative evangelical churches.[2]

---

1. C. Kirk Hadaway and David A. Roozen, *Rerouting the Protestant Mainstream: Sources of Growth and Opportunities for Change* (Nashville: Abingdon Press, 1995).

2. Denominations differ in their relative proportions of growing, plateaued, and declining churches. Half of the churches in most denominations are plateaued—even in growing, conservative, evangelical denominations. When declining churches are added to plateaued churches, the total is well over fifty percent in these denominations.

If we decide not to write off our plateaued and declining churches we are faced with the problem of what to do about them. The problem is one of change, or better yet, transformation. As it turns out, the church in Pennsylvania is more fortunate than most because its regional judicatory has a "Minister of Transformation" on staff whose job it is to help struggling churches change. Her position is unique, as far as I know, and it is an indication that this judicatory is not content with its traditional role of placement, programming, and "putting out fires."

THE FUTURE IS A MOVING TARGET

Some years ago Lyle Schaller, the preeminent church consultant of this generation, remarked, "There seems to be a growing amount of evidence that next year is going to be 1991. If that's true, we've got problems. If it were going to be 1951, we might know what to do."[3] His point was not that our hindsight is better than our foresight, but rather that our religious institutions are "tooled" for an earlier era. And in a context of rapid social change, the problems of any organization can be diagnosed in terms of failure to keep up with the culture.[4] So whether next year is 1991, 2001, or 2011, our primary problem is always perceived in the same way.

Institutions that come to believe that they are behind the times are compelled to answer the question: "What changes can we make that will help us catch up?" In developing a list of possible changes, a consultant or a long-range planning committee may begin with a blank flip chart and a fresh felt-tip marker, but the likely directions for planned change are very limited. Today, most of the suggested strategies for congregational modernization involve acceptance of worship techniques pioneered by independent "seeker-sensitive churches" such as the Willow Creek Community Church: contemporary Christian choruses projected on a screen, a Christian rock band, drama presentations, celebration services, videos, conversational preaching aided by PowerPoint, and con-

---

3. Mark Wingfield, "Get Ready for the Nineties, Not the Fifties, Schaller Tells Churches," *Capital Baptist* (28 June 1990): 3.

4. See Paul F. Salipante and Karen Golden-Biddle, "Managing Traditionality and Strategic Change in Nonprofit Organizations," *Nonprofit Management and Leadership* 6, no. 1 (1995): 23–35.

sumer-oriented marketing techniques. Ten years ago, the strategies predominantly suggested for modernizing the church were considerably different—and ten years from now they will have changed again. The point is that the available options for change are limited if the goal of a directionless, tradition-bound church is to catch up with the culture or with other churches that are more successful in the current religious marketplace.

Older churches are most likely to feel the need to catch up, particularly when they reach the point where they must either do something different or die. Yet the options available to them may require the adoption of procedures so radically different from current practices that acceptance of them may be difficult and conflict about them may be likely. The problem is compounded if it takes a long time to make the prescribed changes. New contextual realities may emerge requiring a solution that is not the one chosen—and the church is back to where it started, out of step and behind the times.

Your church may be in the process of deciding whether or not to use gospel choruses on overhead transparencies for congregational singing, rather than traditional hymns, in the hope of catching up with the megachurches, the desires of your members, or the imagined preferences of the unchurched in your community. Indeed, many people do like this type of worship and want their churches to transform the typical "boring" service into something more upbeat. My parents—who are in their 70s—choose to attend a church in Southern California that has two informal worship services (and one more traditional). They clap their hands along with the younger members of the church as the congregation's band rocks out gospel choruses at the 8:00 A.M. service. This approach may work in their laid-back, conservative-Baptist, California-beach-community church, but in other congregations the same effort comes off as incongruous and strained. I also attended a large Baptist church in Alabama that tried to provide something for everyone by using gospel choruses on a projection screen, a robed choir, and a full orchestra. The orchestra was professional, the choir was excellent, but the choruses didn't seem to fit. As I looked around at people in nearby pews, I noticed that few actually sang the words projected behind the baptistery. They let the choir do it for them.

What happens when consumer taste for the present form of contemporary worship wanes? If your church is not doing worship like this now, it is likely that by the time your church adopts such a modern approach, it will seem cliché to church shoppers. What will you do then? Try something new that is touted as the next wave of the future for contemporary Christian worship? Independent evangelical churches are now talking about the value of liturgy and ritual.[5] Maybe mainline churches are already ahead of the next wave.

The future is a moving target. When we try to catch up with it, we find that we are always one step behind. When we try to anticipate its direction and arrive before it, we find that it has eluded us. How then do we deal with change?

I would argue that trying to figure out what the future holds for churches is not the way. Futurists attempt to envision the future so that we can prepare for it now. Their efforts may be useful, but not for their accuracy in pointing out which specific direction our society is heading. Instead, their value is in preparing us for change.

In order to prepare for change, we must first accept the inevitability of change. We cannot anticipate the changes that will affect us, nor can we plan ahead effectively for the challenges they bring. But we can embrace the naturalness of change and escape the resistance/catch-up, resistance/catch-up cycle in which most churches find themselves enmeshed.

STAYING THE SAME IS NOT THE SAME AS NOT CHANGING

Perhaps instead of trying to change, churches should remain the same. But don't churches do a good job of staying the same anyway? Actually, they do not. All organizations are in a state of constant evolution, as members and leaders grow older, move out, move in, and as the group necessarily adjusts to a changing context. What many organizations do is conform to a self-created image of "the way things ought to be done around here." Static, traditional institutions are all around us, and many churches are of this type, but their static nature is only an illusion. All organizations are in the process of becoming something different—new social incarnations—even as they try to hold on to their most cherished traditions.

---

5. For instance, in 1999 my parents' church added the Apostles Creed to their contemporary services—sung as a chorus. Also see Lamar Boschman, "Worship Megatrends," *Ministries Today* (January/February 1996): 51.

Historical studies have shown that many of our "traditions" are neither as old nor as traditional as we think. Most, in fact, are artificial creations, myths, that we use to make people think that they have lost some idyllic past.[6] The implication always is that we need to reclaim what was lost. As a result, groups spend a great deal of time and energy trying to recover something that *never was* by creating new obligations.

The problem of trying to reclaim an idealized past is endemic to older congregations. Long-term members can tell you about a golden age when the nursery was full and young people crowded church halls. Pictures of huge confirmation classes in the halls prove the point and suggest that something isn't right today. Current problems are blamed on the fact that the church doesn't do things the way they once did them—that their church has become something less than it once was. Such congregations do change, but the direction of change is always toward trying to recreate the church as it is remembered. Older members suggest that the church should renovate its nursery or start a youth program. A pastor may institute a weekly children's sermon even though only a handful of children attend worship.

Churches are blamed for being oriented to the past. But they really are not. They are oriented to a past *ideal*, which they can never recreate. Backward-looking churches appear to be static, but in reality they are in constant flux, trying to follow guidelines that are required by their ideal self-image.

A few years ago I read Michael Crichton's *The Lost World*. From the standpoint of plot, it was a rather predictable sequel to *Jurassic Park*. Still, all of its references to complexity theory, chaos theory, and recent understandings of behavioral evolution fascinated me. In one chapter, for instance, the term "Red Queen phenomenon" is introduced to illustrate how change and adaptation occur even when no change is apparent: "In *Alice in Wonderland*, the Red Queen tells Alice she has to run as fast as she can just to stay where she is."[7] Like Alice, churches (and many other organizations) are running as hard as they can just to stay were they are—trying to do ministry in the same way, but under changing circumstances.[8]

---

6. Eric Hobsbawm and Terence Ranger, eds., *The Invention of Tradition* (Cambridge: Cambridge University Press, 1983).

7. Michael Crichton, *The Lost World* (New York: Alfred A. Knopf, 1995), 173. Also see Niles Eldredge, "Evolution and Environment: The Two Faces of Biodiversity," *Natural History* (June 1998): 54.

8. They are trying to remain the same, very particular incarnation rather than following the principle of incarnation—which implies continuous change and growth.

Change is inevitable, and the church *is* changing, regardless of its efforts to remain unchanged. The problem is that what we are trying to maintain isn't real. We are attempting to preserve an idealized set of traditional forms and normative practices.[9] In doing so, we keep ourselves from making changes that might be more adaptive if the changes were to occur more naturally. The same situation is true, I might add, if the direction of our efforts is to create a utopian (rather than traditional) ideal church. We are doomed to failure, just like all of the failed attempts to create an ideal society through social engineering. The church, like society, has problems that are unsolvable and, therefore, permanent. They are not technical glitches that can be fixed.[10] As Robert J. Samuelson notes in reference to domestic problems such as crime and poverty, "they may get better or worse, but they don't go away." [11] Creating an ideal church, an ideal society, an ideal marriage, an ideal social group of any kind is not possible because they always will have problems that can only "get better or worse."

Our churches must change, but not by trying to keep up or by trying to create or maintain structures and processes that are consistent with our ideal images of what a church should be. The most innovative organizations do not change by anticipating the future. They change by *creating* the future.[12] One way they do this is by being open to innovation occurring outside their boundaries. But more important is their openness to ideas that emerge from within—from their own people—as resolute action naturally leads to new possibilities. I should add, however, that openness does not mean mindless acceptance of new things. It means the willingness to consider new possibilities without immediately passing judgment. Even if we decide not to rip out our church organs, install video

---

9. Discourse about the necessity for identifying and holding onto "core values" is a very clear example of ideal-seeking. The inherent goodness of these ideals is not disputed, only the impossibility of reaching and maintaining them.

10. See Ronald A. Heifetz, *Leadership without Easy Answers* (Cambridge: Belknap Press of Harvard University Press, 1994).

11. Robert J. Samuelson, *The Good Life and Its Discontents: The American Dream in the Age of Entitlement 1945–1995* (New York: Times Books, 1996), 29.

12. See Paul C. Light, *Sustaining Innovation: Creating Nonprofit and Government Organizations That Innovate Naturally* (San Francisco: Jossey-Bass, 1998). Also see James C. Collins and Jerry I. Porras, *Built to Last: Successful Habits of Visionary Companies* (New York: HarperBusiness, 1994).

screens, sing medieval polyphony, encourage "holy laughter," or any number of other possible adaptations, we should be able to learn from the fact that some churches are doing these things—and are finding them to be meaningful and exciting.

THE PROBLEM OF GOAL DISPLACEMENT

Churches can change by remaining the same, but churches cannot remain the same until they realize what business they are in.

Any organization that is successful in that it has been able to thrive for more than a few years, develops a useful set of customs, norms, practices, and structures. These cultural patterns are developed early in an organization's life cycle in direct response to the environment in which the organization lives. New organizations die easily, including churches—as church "planters" in all denominations will attest. Once an organization reaches a point of stability, however—in that it is not constantly concerned about whether or not it will make it—a subtle shift begins to take place in the way the group adapts. The primary impetus for change then comes primarily from within rather than from without. Life within the organization becomes more of a concern to group members than the group's relationship with the outside world.

What occurs is called *goal displacement*—a process by which the primary mission of an organization is replaced by operative goals that have little, if anything, to do with the organization's original reason for being. In almost all cases, the new goals involve a focus on group maintenance and member satisfaction—particularly involving the satisfaction of group leaders and core members.

The old story of the "lifesaving club" that was started with the purpose of rescuing shipwreck victims, but then evolved into a social club, is applicable here. It provides an apt illustration of goal displacement. Other good examples abound in industry, government, social service organizations, and also in Dilbert cartoons. Many churches which began as lifesaving clubs for their community slowly become more like clans, gangs, or social clubs through goal displacement. They forget why they exist and what they are for. It should be noted, however, that this evolution is rarely the result of conscious decisions to change the purpose and operational goals of an organization. Goal displacement occurs as current members try to maintain a group character that they find personally fulfilling. If a certain activity meets their needs, they try to maintain it and, over time, it develops a certain sense of "oughtness." As more and more group practices become traditional and meaningful only to current members, the group may lose its original purpose or mission. It also cuts itself off from potential new members—persons who might be interested in the group's organizing purpose, but not in what it has become.[13]

Goal displacement and the tendency to maintain an idealized image of group life happens to all churches—liberal and conservative. The transition to this state is natural, gradual, and has a lot to do with the fact that religion in the Western world exists in congregational form. Congregations are a classic example of groups where the primary value of belonging is in what the member gains through the character of the interaction itself—through participation in group activities. "Obligatory groups," as social theorist Michael Hechter calls them, may originate with heroic religious goals (reaching the world for Christ; creating a path to enlightenment), but since they would not exist without the enjoyment and sense of belonging members gain from their interactions with fellow members, it is very easy for such groups to forget about their original mission (or at least take it for granted) and focus on providing a rewarding social environment for their members.[14] In other words, they become good social clubs, but not-so-good churches. And as good social clubs, churches can survive and even thrive if they remain sufficiently accepting of new members and if the form of belonging they offer is valued by the people in the local community. When the culture or the immediate community context changes, however, a church may suffer because the needs of its current members are no longer identical to those of potential recruits.

In North America there are more than enough good social clubs, but not nearly enough good churches. Some might disagree, but I think British sociologist Bryan Wilson's characterization of American churches as largely secularized is quite accurate.[15] A secularized church may be labeled a reli-

---

13. Churches and most other nonprofit organizations were created to do something worthwhile—not to provide congenial social settings for group members. Churches, universities and hospitals were not designed to be social clubs. A group's purpose may evolve legitimately in the direction of doing something worthwhile that is not exactly the same as its organizing purpose.

14. Michael Hechter, *Principles of Group Solidarity* (Berkeley: University of California Press, 1987).

15. Bryan R. Wilson, *Religion in Secular Society* (London: C. A. Watts, 1966).

gious organization by society, but a religious label does not mean that much of what takes place there is religious. What is a religious institution? Although opinions differ greatly on this matter, I accept the definition that religious institutions are those that connect or relate the everyday world (the immanent) to a reality that is behind, beyond, or subsumes our world (the transcendent).[16] Religious institutions allow the individual to experience transcendent reality in the midst of everyday existence. *Communion* is another way of expressing how churches facilitate this participation. It results in what Sallie McFague calls "an embodied form of knowing."[17] We know God and God's earthly reality because we have experienced both in transfigured form. If this sort of experience is not a part of a church, then one could say that the church is not really religious.

If we use an immanent/transcendent definition of religion, it follows that many churches in the United States, Canada, and the rest of the Western world are not very religious. Western rationalism, in general, and Protestantism, in particular, militates against the experience of the mystery of God. Mainstream Protestant churches often intellectualize the connection between the transcendent and the immanent; conservative evangelical churches tend to replace God's mystery with mechanistic formulae and causal logic. These are extreme statements, of course, but where in North American Christianity does one see much emphasis on mystery, the spirit, religious experience, or communion with God? These are probably most evident among Roman Catholic, Orthodox, Anglican, Episcopal, Pentecostal Holiness, African American, and some Unitarian Universalist churches. Even the rapidly growing seeker-sensitive megachurches seem to have little that is religious in their worship. Most combine moral lessons and self-help in an entertaining package. Not much mystery there![18]

---

16. Even though the definition seems a bit dualistic, it also would seem to fit Eastern, "nonreligious" religions like Zen Buddhism or Taoism if the immanent world is understood as the world as seen through the categories of social convention.

17. Sallie McFague, *The Body of God: An Ecological Theology* (Minneapolis: Fortress Press, 1993), 28.

18. The argument that such churches hide their committed, religiously meaningful underside is not very convincing because what is hidden tends only to be a variation of the overly rational faith of conservative evangelicalism. A legalistic, rule-bound god is not a god of mystery, and thus is not a real god.

THE DRUCKER QUESTION

Peter Drucker has spent much of his working life asking corporations and other organizations the same question: "What is your business?"[19] When firms take his question seriously, they often realize that they do not know what their business is. They may manufacture tennis balls, for example, but is doing so their business? Their real business may be to maximize shareholder profits, give the owner something to do, provide a good living for their employees, or drive out the competition. But these firms also may realize that their true business has more to do with health and physical fitness than with tennis. In fact, one major study demonstrated that the business of corporations that were successful over many years was not in producing a specific product, but to meet a specific need in society.[20] The product they are producing is simply a way to meet that need.

Churches should ask themselves, "What business are we in?" And once they (re)discover their business, they should stick to it. This is what I mean by trying to stay the same. Our mission is to focus on our purpose, and we achieve that mission by resolute action in the here and now. If we are consistent in our efforts to remain what we are, even in changing circumstances, the changes that we make in what we do will always be consistent with our purpose.

Essentially, what we want to be (continually become or incarnate) is an organization with the capacity to fulfill (continually accomplish) our *purpose*. Our *mission* is to do just that. What we are—our specific incarnation at any point in time—is the appropriate means at the present moment to do what needs to be done, given the substance of our purpose.[21]

It often happens that what an organization does has little to do with its purpose. Many churches have mission statements, but how much of what we do helps to fulfill, actualize, or live out our purpose? Most of our efforts are directed toward satisfying one another, blaming someone for our problems, congratulating ourselves, reinforcing an unrealistic self-identity, or simply enjoying being together. The true purpose of the church has been subverted. Its purpose now is to maintain itself as a cohesive social group

---

19. Peter F. Drucker, *The Five Most Important Questions You Will Ever Ask about Your Nonprofit Organization* (San Francisco: Jossey-Bass, 1993), 11.

20. Collins and Porras, *Built to Last*, 31.

21. A description of our incarnation may be expressed through an identity statement.

while at the same time shoring up its identity as a place where people worship God, learn the Bible, and maybe even help the needy and oppressed.

WHAT IS OUR PURPOSE?

What should be the unchanging purpose of any church? Your specific identity as a congregation will vary, of course, depending on who your members are and how you understand the implications of your mission. But let's begin at a more basic level.

What distinguishes the purpose of a church from that of a for-profit corporation, or even from a social club? I prefer straightforward language, so I will turn again to a statement from Peter Drucker: "The business of a church is to change people; the business of a corporation is to satisfy them."[22] This is, I believe, a statement that should be taken to heart by every church leader. It forces each of us to ask the question, "are people being changed (transformed) in my congregation?" If the answer is no, then my church has a different purpose, and that purpose probably is to satisfy people.

Of course, to change people or transform them begs the question of what they should be changed into. The obvious answer is that they should be changed into disciples who are open to the spirit of God and live a life of faith, vocation, and reconciliation in God's Realm. Thus, the transformation is intentional and directed, rather than haphazard. It also is embodied and incarnational. People change, because all things change, but in most cases the church isn't much of an ingredient for personal change, much less the catalyst. The church can be both a *catalyst for transformation*, as people experience God through transcendent worship, and a *place of formation*, as people become part of a community of faith.

---

22. Paraphrased from "Managing to Minister: An Interview with Peter Drucker," *Leadership* (spring quarter 1989): 16.

Chapter two

VISIONS, VOWS, AND PURPOSE

Be wary of aims set too extreme and plans too vast
—Stanley Herman[1]

SOMETIMES WE ARE IN TOO MUCH of a hurry. We want to do God's work now! Or our problems seem so severe that we don't take the time to look more closely at ourselves. Many churches see that the fields are white with harvest and feel compelled to mobilize the troops to get the harvest in. For other churches, the fields are just as ripe, but their combine is broken and they don't have the money to fix it. Maybe the bank is threatening to foreclose. When faced with unlimited opportunity or paralyzing problems, organizations often make bad decisions, based on an inaccurate reading of the situation. They lack vision—a sense of perception—that comes only when they look at who they are and what they are doing from a different vantage point.

What is the state of the harvest in your community? Are the fields ripe? When we look closely, we notice an odd thing about these fields—they are always white with harvest. Maybe we need to get to work, but maybe we don't need to be in such a hurry. And if the combine is broken, perhaps we can find some other way to bring in the harvest. In such fields, it is enough to begin the harvest, to start the process that leads to transformation. So what if the laborers are few? The transformational ministry of the church produces disciples. We are harvesting laborers to work with us in fields that are perpetually ripe.

---

1. Stanley M. Herman, *The Tao at Work: On Leading and Following* (San Francisco: Jossey-Bass, 1994), 52.

CATCH A CASTED VISION

In a *Christian Ministry* article titled "We Are Called to Be God's Prophets," John Robert McFarland decried congregational efforts to emulate industry:

> We have unquestioningly adopted the model of CEO or entrepreneur of the congregation, seeing the church as an organization that must be run like a business, viewing members as customers and other churches as competitors, pursuing church growth instead of performing evangelism, and budget raising instead of stewardship. The bottom line is financial not spiritual . . . it's a business understanding of the church. The people of God are either owners or customers—but not disciples.[2]

When compared to corporations like Microsoft, Proctor and Gamble, or Home Depot, the church seems like a weak institution that doesn't get much done. Like the family farm or the corner grocery, is the day of the neighborhood church done? According to many religious observers, this is now the day of the vision-directed megachurch, organized to provide programs tailored to the changing religious needs of postmodern consumers. Such churches get a lot done and serve a lot of people. With armies of volunteers and top-notch equipment, the megachurches seem to harvest a lot more wheat.

Recognizing the need to get more done, books on church leadership ask churches to do what they think corporations do: Work toward actualizing the vision dreamed by a CEO and cast to his company.[3] According to Norman Shawchuck and Roger Heuser, "The church must live out of a vision, which originates with the senior pastor and leaders."[4] It is a top-down strategy for vitalizing a congregation that demands that a minister develop and sell a compelling vision of what the organization can become. A vision offers an alternative future that can be realized if members work together, move in a single direction, with each eye on the same prize.

---

2. John Robert McFarland, "We Are Called to Be God's Prophets," *The Christian Ministry* (September/October 1998): 34–35.

3. Alan E. Nelson, *Leading Your Ministry: A Moment of Insight Is Worth a Lifetime of Experience* (Nashville: Abingdon Press, 1996): 35.

4. Norman Shawchuck and Roger Heuser, *Leading the Congregation: Caring for Yourself while Serving Others* (Nashville: Abingdon Press, 1993), 114.

What happens to visions in the real world? Many corporations find that visionary leadership is not the answer to their prayers. As Peter Senge observes, "many firms that have jumped on the 'vision bandwagon' in recent years have found that lofty vision alone fails to turn around a firm's fortunes."[5] Some churches are finding out the same thing—the hard way.

A minister once cast a vision to build what he called "the greatest church" in his city. He pastored a medium-sized Baptist church in an older suburban area of a large southern city. I will call the church "Big Hope Baptist." The church was growing—quite rapidly in fact—and its worship services were so packed that many people had to stand. Church members, who were attracted by the pastor's teaching ministry or to the Christian rock outreach program, were enthusiastic about the church and excited about its future. A larger sanctuary and more educational space were needed, but rather than expand at their present site, the pastor's vision called for a huge new worship center and a Christian high school to serve the entire city. Despite financial obstacles and the opinion of many that the church was attempting the impossible, a large tract of land was purchased, a combination worship center and school was built, and the congregation moved to its new home.

In most books of this genre you might expect that the church grew quite rapidly and actually became the greatest church in that city. It didn't. The church never grew again and struggled to meet its enormous mortgage payments. The high school did very well, however, and eventually became organizationally separate from the church and bought out the congregation's interest in the property. The church that "would be the greatest" took the money from its settlement and built a new, much more modest, facility where it now meets.

There are many practical reasons why Big Hope Baptist failed to realize its pastor's vision. It was a younger, blue-collar and middle-class congregation with contemporary Christian music, pastored by a non-seminary educated minister who preached expository sermons—slowly and methodically working his way through books of the Bible Sunday morning and evening. Big Hope Baptist moved to an extremely wealthy suburban area and into a facility so large that it seemed to swallow up the congregation. It could at-

---

5. Peter M. Senge, *The Fifth Discipline: The Art and Practice of the Learning Organization* (New York: Doubleday, 1990), 12.

tract none of the affluent residents from this new local context, and the exciting crush of bodies in the old facility was replaced by the hollowness of a sanctuary no more than one-third full. The church failed to capitalize on its new building and is by no means alone in its failure to do so. Most churches that build for future growth do not grow. They decline. The "if we build it they will come" strategy of church growth does not work.[6] Most congregations tend to relax after they accomplish a major goal, such as a building program, and fail to sustain the level of effort necessary even to remain stable.

The members of Big Hope Baptist did not relax so much as they were dazed. The church just didn't feel the same. They lost their sense of excitement. When the church stopped growing, the pastor preached even harder about evangelism. Members got tired of hearing about it and began to criticize the pastor and "his" new building. People said it was too large, the colors were strange, and some of the structural elements and fixtures did not fit their idea of what a church should look like. The charismatic leader lost his hold on his followers and many began to drift away and join other congregations. Plateau turned into decline.

If a vision is so important for the success of a congregation, then why did such a vision-oriented church make so many wrong decisions and fail so miserably? The answer is that it was a misguided vision, as most visions are. Visions excite and motivate, but they often lead in the wrong direction because "they do not account for the way things are."[7] Typically, they are too specific, too unrealistic, and the charismatic leaders who promote them are too driven and personally persuasive to permit much change in what they see as God's plan. When something is preordained by God, reality seems irrelevant. But as Bernard Glassman and Rick Fields warn, "reality has a way of sneaking up on us. It will always win in the end."[8]

---

6. Some churches who build new, larger sanctuaries do grow, of course. This happens when they build in order to do more of what it was that led to their growth. When churches envision a new building as the answer to their problems or as symbolic of having "made it," they typically plateau or decline.

7. Alan Briskin, *The Stirring of Soul in the Workplace* (San Francisco: Berrett-Koeler, 1998), 237.

8. Bernard Glassman and Rick Fields, *Instructions to the Cook: A Zen Master's Lessons in Living a Life That Matters* (New York: Bell Tower, 1996).

FACING REAL PROBLEMS

Among mainline churches, the more typical situation is the troubled church in need of a *savior*. Rather than opportunities, they only see grim realities. Many mainline churches are declining and some have reached the point where their survival is in question. This situation is also widespread in business and politics.[9] What do churches, businesses, towns, and nations do when they are facing ruin? They call for someone to save them. According to Ronald Heifetz, "In a crisis we tend to look for the wrong kind of leadership. We call for someone with answers, decisions, strength, and a map of the future, someone who knows where we ought to be going—in short, someone who can make hard problems simple."[10] Declining and conflict-ridden churches want the wrong kind of leader. They even may pressure their pastor to start acting like the wrong kind of leader.

At a consultation a few years ago with Unitarian Universalist ministers, a newly called pastor told me that the lay leaders of her church had given her a free hand to change anything that needed to be changed. She had been hired to attract new people so the church could grow, get out of its financial mess, and build a new building. Church leaders wanted a charismatic pastor with a vision for growth. They wanted her to be their savior. I told her that if the strategy didn't work, she might be out of a job, and if it *did* work she would have a troupe of followers, rather than a church. It was a short-sighted, quick fix strategy for change.

Working together toward a promised vision may give a renewed purpose to the members of a congregation. When people are excited and motivated, and when they are doing purposeful work, they will feel better about their situation even if underlying problems are not being addressed. A heroic vision only exacerbates underlying problems and undermines the ability of the congregation to work on them. A heroic vision presents a simple solution to a problem that cannot easily be fixed. Hard problems are not simple; they are hard! Making our problems appear to be simple and working on simple solutions keeps us from working on real solutions.

Following a visionary leader also changes the nature of the church. To the extent that a leader captures the imagination of her congregation, the

---

9. See Ronald A. Heifetz's excellent book, *Leadership without Easy Answers* (Cambridge: Belknap Press of Harvard University Press, 1994).

10. Ibid., 2.

church is transformed from a community into a band of followers. A community has the capacity to work together to solve real problems. A band of followers does not. They can only follow the dictates of their leader. But this is not true leadership. Leadership is about getting people to face their problems—"problems for which there are not simple, painless solutions."[11]

FROM VISIONS TO PRODUCTS AND SERVICES

A vision is a preconceived reality that is "out there"—ready to be realized through goal-directed action. It is an earthly version of pie in the sky for which we don't have to wait to get by and by. We can get it now if we are willing to work hard enough. A vision motivates because it suggests that we can become something better. More than a reward, a vision imagines a new state of being, in which both organizational identity and outcomes will be transformed. Problems will be solved, and we can live into a glorious new future.

But visions never actually become reality—including those that are seen as successes—because visions are ideal constructions. The problem is similar to the one discussed in the previous chapter in which congregations try to conform to an ideal conception of what a church should be like, or when a congregation tries to recreate a past golden age. Whether it is a golden past, a perfect present or a utopian future, such churches are trying to create an ideal rather than to be something that is real.

Rather than creating a community with a life of its own, a visionary leader creates something that must be sustained through great effort. The situation reminds me of Las Vegas, Nevada, which came into being through the vision of Bugsy Siegal and is sustained by offering gambling and other forms of live entertainment to visitors. Las Vegas could not survive as a major city without the gambling industry, and in an effort to keep it going and to counter threats from Atlantic City, Biloxi, and a host of other newer gambling venues, the hotels get bigger and the casinos become ever more elaborate.

All goal-directed organizations face the same dilemma eventually—how do we keep it going? How do we keep people motivated and working after our vision fades following its success or failure? Visionary movements that

---

11. Ibid.

survive do so because they evolve into service-providing organizations. They offer goods to patrons in exchange for their participation. Service-oriented churches offer spiritual food and patrons give their money and time in order to keep the institution going. In the face of competition, they offer more services, meet more "felt needs," build larger, more elaborate facilities and thereby keep their patrons hooked.

But the product of the church is not the services it provides. Quality worship, supportive community, and social justice ministries are not bait we use to attract people and keep them in church. Offering ministries as consumable goods in order to "feed" members changes the nature of the organization and undermines the purpose of the system. The product of the church is transformed lives—not quality ministry. Ministries help transform people and provide channels for living transformed lives.

A GOOD PLACE TO START

Calling a visionary pastor is the wrong place for a church to begin. Trying to generate a vision is the wrong place for a pastor to start. The best thing to do is to confront the issue of organizational purpose. What we should ask is "what is a church?" Then we should ask, "why is this church here?" In other words, why don't we close our doors, sell our building, and disperse our members to other local churches that seem to be having fewer problems? Do we have some reason for being other than the fact that we have always been here and our members feel at home? If not, then we really don't have a purpose other than continuance or survival. We are a club that happens to hold worship services, led by a pastor serving as "clan priest."

If we rediscover that the purpose of our church is to transform people— to bring down their self-constructed walls, dissolve their delusions, and help them see God—then we also have a mission. That mission is to be a church that actualizes our purpose in a way unique to our congregation. It is to form a transformational community. We incarnate (through our gifts and vocations) a system or open "vessel" in which our purpose is worked out.[12]

The primary purpose of the church is to be the church—not to try to become something that it is not, however wonderful that new something

---

12. Our *identity*, therefore, is a description of the way we currently incarnate the vessel that realizes our purpose. Our mission is to use what we are at the present time to create the best vessel possible.

might seem.[13] Being oneself, and growing from there, implies doing something, of course, but our focus should not be on achieving goals or measuring output. If a corporation is like a machine that produces a product, then the church is like a person who is here on earth to live. A major part of life involves purposeful action—taking care of the necessary tasks. The problem occurs when we transform these tasks into goals, acquisitions, and accomplishments. Life can become a never-ending struggle to accumulate things or to live up to someone's unrealistic expectations (our own or others).[14]

Individuals and churches should look at their lives in terms of calling. Who are we? What are we called to do? What are we compelled to do? By doing what we are called to do, starting with where we are, we give our lives meaning. I was trained as a sociologist, and I also love the church. My calling is to study churches and to help churches, church leaders, and mission organizations. That is why I am writing this book at home on a rainy Saturday morning, rather than drinking coffee with friends at the corner coffeehouse or watching ESPN. Writing isn't a lot of fun. I also don't have to do it for my job. Why do I do it? Obviously, I want to help churches through my writing, but the odd thing is, I do it best when I don't think about the effect it might have on others. I do it best when I follow my compulsion, and I just do it.

For the church, a sense of mission and purpose should be even clearer than it is for me as an individual, because, after all, being a church implies a more specific reason for being. At base, a church is (or should be) a worshiping community where people are transformed into citizens of God's Realm, into people who see differently and, thus, live differently in the world. In order to be churches, all churches should be that. How they worship, form community, and transform their members will differ. But the doing of these things is always connected to their basic purpose as churches.

If a church's mission is directed at its purpose and its members are being transformed through that mission, the congregation can and should dream about doing great things (ministries) that are in keeping with its purpose and unfolding incarnation. A mission (to actualize purpose) should be "like a compass that shows us the direction to go in and that keeps us on course."[15]

---

13. See McFarland, "We Are Called to Be God's Prophets," 34–35.

14. See Parker J. Palmer, *Let Your Life Speak: Listening for the Voice of Vocation* (San Francisco: Jossey-Bass, 2000), 10–12

15. Glassman and Fields, *Instructions to the Cook*, 17

There also is no reason why a church must be limited by its current tools, personnel, and resources to do great things. There are no limits to dreaming, but we should not confuse our dreams with specific, possible realities. That is why I use the term *vow* rather than *vision* for desired outcomes. A vow is an intention to do something great that emerges from working out our purpose. It is not a specific goal or a targeted, idealized destination. It is a compulsion that suggests specific achievable things (objectives). Because of what we are (our specific incarnation as a transformational vessel), we decide to do important things—and then we do them.

All Saints Episcopal Church in Pasadena, California, provides an excellent example of how a vow emerges. Being a vessel of transformation necessarily involves stewardship, but in the case of All Saints, stewardship is "not just of our body, not just of our relationships, not just of our church, but of the *world* [emphasis added]."[16] Stewardship of the world is expressed as caring, helping ministries and good works, but it also involves working for justice as a way of transforming the world—to spread the reign of God. What they call their job and what I call a vow is this: "On behalf of Jesus Christ to dismantle all structures of injustice."[17] Dismantling injustice is not a vision or a corporate goal—it is an intention and a direction that leads to specific actions. It is a vow, even a "covenant" with the world. Rather than following a vision, we give ourselves vision—the ability to see—and then we act accordingly (and resolutely).

---

16. Patrick McNamara, *More Than Money: Portraits of Transformative Stewardship* (Bethesda, Md.: Alban Institute, 1999), 98.

17. Ibid.

Chapter three

FROM PROGRAM PLANS TO "VIRTUOUS CYCLES"

WHAT IS A CHURCH? Despite our lip service about a church being people, the members of a congregation, we tend to look at the church like we do all other organizations—in terms of its structural elements. Constitutions, bylaws, staff positions, committees, councils, boards, sessions, budgets, missions, ministries and programs seem to form the substance of the church. All churches have organizational structure and most have a lot more than they need.[1]

Within our church walls, we try to build an organizational structure that is just as solid. Our denomination may even supply an organizational plan that lays out a blueprint for what our internal structure should look like. This is not necessarily a bad thing—if such plans are taken as guidelines rather than as mandatory requirements. Without them we might forget something essential or continue doing something foolish (such as allowing the treasurer to take the Sunday offering home and count it on her kitchen table).[2]

The danger in trying to build a properly functioning church by setting up the correct committee structure, policies, staffing patterns, and programs is that once they are in place, we assume the work of the church is being done. But is it? Just as the building only provides the space to contain the church as organization, the organization only provides a framework to guide the life and work of the congregation.[3] Within this framework, what

---

1. Churches tend to accumulate excessive structure over time. A moderately large Presbyterian church in Birmingham, Alabama, had one hundred twenty separate standing committees before its interim pastor helped them reduce the number to only twenty.

2. Structure should enable an organization by creating a safe space in which to work. It should not constrain our movements. It is like a pilot's checklist or a set of building codes. They prevent disaster, but do not determine how we should fly or the shape of our building.

3. Stanley M. Herman, *The Tao at Work: On Leading and Following* (San Francisco: Jossey-Bass, 1994), 38.

exactly is happening? Is it a place where people come to socialize or are their lives being changed? Focusing on getting the right structure creates a "purpose vacuum" which people naturally fill with purposes of their own.[4]

If the church we build seems to be operating efficiently—programs are running smoothly, people are joining, money is coming in—there will be no reason to examine it very closely. Still, because organizations always want to do a better job, they may add a few more good things each year. Usually, these additions take the form of new programs and ministries. If we have enough money, we might add new staff or program space. Lay leaders might think that a family life center would bring more young families to the church. An overworked minister, with responsibilities for Christian education and youth, might suggest that the church add a youth minister. Denominational offices load our churches with even more programs, each one more important than the next. Literature from Boston, Chicago, Cleveland, Louisville, Nashville, New York, and Toronto often goes unopened to avoid hearing about the latest program that all churches *must* add.

Ezra Earl Jones maintains that "piling on activities is an addiction in the United Methodist Church . . . we know how to list our needs, plan programs to respond, and sometimes we follow them through. Nothing changes." His lament is not limited to United Methodism. All denominational agencies and publishing houses do the same thing. Churches select some programs, ignore others, add a few of their own, and groan under the weight of what they have agreed to do. The result is a mishmash of largely disconnected programs, some of which are "worked" hard and others that receive little attention. Few things are dropped, of course. The tendency is to add more and more over time. They seem like good programs, so we should adopt them as our own. But just because we make a decision and put a program in place does not mean that it will produce the desired outcome. Here is an example.

The long-range planning committee of a large church in Nashville, Tennessee, once developed a plan for neighborhood "cell groups" that would assume the task of member oversight from its board of deacons. A plan was drawn up, discussed, revised, recommended by the church council, approved at the monthly business meeting, and assigned to the minister of education and the nominating committee for implementation. After about six months, a program director was enlisted. After several more months,

---

4. Structural solutions for fixing organizational problems only create new voids.

neighborhood group leaders were recruited, and after a few weeks, members were assigned to groups. Some of the groups began to meet, and when a big snowstorm canceled Sunday worship services, members were encouraged to attend the neighborhood groups instead. But after a year the neighborhood group program was abandoned—although not officially. No vote was taken; the program just died.

A plan was made. There was an official vote to implement it. A director was appointed and empowered. Still, little happened and the program was never fully realized and died a premature death. Why? No one was really interested in the program—particularly the ministerial staff of the church. It was just another program developed by a committee that had to be staffed. There was nothing particularly wrong with the program, or the plan to implement it, but without the commitment of staff and laity to make it a central ministry of the church, it became just one more ministry amidst a wagonload of other ministries the church carried.

Whether through planning or gathering "ministry moss," the organizational structure of the church tends to become more and more complex, overburdened, and unwieldy. Some churches add so many committees that the number of positions to be filled exceeds the number of adult church members. Standing committees meet each month and talk about their responsibilities, but never do anything about them. Planning committees update old plans by adding a column for each successive year and the words "continue, continue, continue." I am not being intentionally cynical; this is what really happens to organizations over time. We create organizational structure and delude ourselves into thinking that we are accomplishing something. Meanwhile, the structure takes on a life of its own and develops the characteristics of a bureaucracy: "an organization put together for a purpose, but coming to survive for its own sake."[5]

Putting the proper structure in place does not ensure that the proper actions occur within the structure, or that the expected outcomes result from our actions. We tend to work on structure when we want to go in a different direction, because structure is tangible and fixing it seems easy. But for churches, structure is much less important than personal relationships and community life. Changing structure or adding new structure may have no noticeable effect on our actions or our results.

---

5. Edward de Bono, *I Am Right, You Are Wrong: From This to the New Renaissance, from Rock Logic to Water Logic* (London: Viking, 1990), 234.

REACTING TO PROBLEMS BY SETTING GOALS

When the structure we put in place seems to be operating efficiently, there is little reason to look at our results too closely. We can assume the proper job is being done. But what happens when it is clear that something is wrong?

For instance, most mainline Protestant denominations are declining in membership. What do we do? We ignore the problem as long as we can. Sometimes we even say we are glad the problem is happening. We didn't need those conservative churches that left; we are only losing the deadwood; our commitments to social justice are more important than membership growth. Occasionally we try to do something about our problems. We vote to establish a new priority or assign a task force to study the situation. One effort to deal with membership losses came in the form of a challenge to the churches published in a judicatory newsletter. The area minister called for "every church [to] increase worship attendance by 5%," "every congregation [to] increase church school enrollment by 10%" and "every congregation [to] experience a NET increase in membership" in the next year. He went on to say, "I believe that these are attainable goals for congregations. There are a number of congregations that will exceed the minimal goals I have suggested. But for other churches, these challenges will take every effort." What happened? Not surprisingly, the judicatory lost members and congregations that year at about the same rate as usual (1.5%). The challenge to work harder failed to turn around area churches because thirty years of membership loss is not a technical problem amenable to a quick fix.[6]

When the structure and programs we put in place don't result in success, the tendency is to resort to goal-setting and corporate planning models. Just like Wal-Mart sets goals for increases in net income, we set goals for net increases in membership. A leader "casts" a challenging vision of a desired future and lays out a strategic plan to bridge the chasm between the current situation and the desired future reality.[7]

---

6. See Ronald A. Heifetz, *Leadership without Easy Answers* (Cambridge: Belknap Press of Harvard University Press, 1994).

7. "The Essence of Strategic Leadership," *Netfax* 28 (18 September 1995): 1, and "Deploying Vision: A Framework for Large-scale Change," *Forum Files* 5, no. 1 (March 1995): 1–2. Both are published by The Leadership Network, Tyler, Tex.

Casting visions is not limited to the heroic leaders of organizations in crisis (as noted in the previous chapter). Non-charismatic leaders in organizations with problems (but no crisis) also may try to mobilize action through vision casting. Doing so is ineffectual because the situation does not seem to call for drastic action. The vision is seen as wishful thinking and is largely ignored.

Because churches by nature have diffuse goals that are hard-to-measure, it is a mistake to try to solve problems by setting specific, easy-to-measure goals. In most cases our efforts to reach them will backfire.[8] Focusing on tangible, instrumental goals—like attracting more members and receiving more money—diverts our attention from our true (diffuse) goals and undermines our ability to reach both types of goals. A successful effort to establish instrumental goals changes the nature of the organization, so that it begins to act more like a for-profit corporation than a church. Corralling more and more people into our churches on Sunday morning is not our purpose. More people do not equal success at reaching our goals. If we do reach more people, that is good, but our real goals should be measured in terms of the impact our churches have on people's lives. Are they being transformed?

Returning to the Drucker question posed in chapter 1, we need to ask, "what is our business?" To illustrate the point, let's compare McDonalds, the Disney Corporation, and the church.

In *Built to Last*, James Collins and Jerry Porras discuss the key characteristics of American companies that have been successful for many decades.[9] One of these companies is Disney and the authors illustrate how new employees are trained to live out the Disney ethos:

Trainer: What business are we in? Everybody knows McDonald's makes hamburgers. What does Disney make?

New Hire: It makes people happy.

Trainer: Yes, exactly! It makes people happy. It doesn't matter who they are, what language they speak, what they do, where they come from, what color they are, or anything else. We're here to make 'em happy. . . . Nobody's been hired for a job. Everybody's been cast for a role in our show.

The business of Disney is to make people happy. It is not to get more people to attend Disney World. The assumption is that if people are made happy then more will come and pay to attend Disney's various theme parks and shows. The philosophy of the Merck Corporation is similarly indirect:

---

8. Even when we seem to succeed in terms of reaching our goals, we will fail because becoming a goal-directed organization alters our true product.

9. James C. Collins and Jerry I. Porras, *Built to Last: Successful Habits of Visionary Companies* (New York: HarperBusiness, 1994), 128.

"Medicine is for the patients; not for the profits. The profits follow."[10] By focusing on a purpose that transcends instrumental goals, successful companies become even more successful.

If Disney makes people happy, what does the church "make"? The goal of more people is similar to the corporate goal of more money—a goal that inevitably leads to corporate failure. So if we are failing at our ancillary goal of growth, we should look first to what we are making. If we adapt the Merck mission and say, "Churches are for the transformation; not for the growth, the growth follows," then lack of growth implies that people are not being changed.

DOING AND NOT ACHIEVING

A good set of programs does not necessarily add up to a good church, and setting goals is not the way to revitalize a church that is foundering. The church is a system that works within a structure. Changing, elaborating, or adding to the structure may not affect the system very much; it may only change the channels through which the same system flows. The results may not change at all, because every system is designed for the results it is getting. If you want different results, you have to redesign the system.[11]

From a systemic perspective, *mainline denominations are systems designed to decline*. In a *Newsweek* article, Stanley Hauerwas was quoted as saying, "God is killing mainline Protestantism in America."[12] But let's not blame it on God. If anyone is doing the killing, it is us. We are killing ourselves.[13] If the current system is designed to lose members, it will not do us any good to try to do a better job at what we are already doing. We are doing a fine job at losing members now and we surely don't want to do even better!

Some of the systemic reasons for our decline are not our fault, of course. The white, middle class, college-educated Americans who make up the overwhelming majority of mainline church membership have a very low birth

---

10. Ibid., 16.

11. Ezra Earl Jones, "The United Methodist Church: Changing the System," (unpublished paper, presented 10 August 1994 in San Bernardino, Calif.).

12. Kenneth L. Woodward, "Dead End for the Mainline?" *Newsweek*, 9 August 1993, 47.

13. Hauerwas probably would agree, because in reference to God killing the mainline he says, "we goddam well deserve it." We do deserve what is happening, because we are doing it.

rate. Calling for young parents in mainline churches to have more children does not seem to be a viable option.[14] The systemic problem we can work on is the fact that at least half of the children reared in mainline churches fail to return to the church after they finish their education. And some of those who do return only do so for a few years in order to expose their children to good Christian values. Without a steady supply of singles and young families, our churches are graying.

We are not losing many members to conservative megachurches. That is a myth fostered by odd examples we read in newspapers or when we hear about someone's son or daughter who finds Jesus in a dramatic way. By and large, the unchurched children of the mainline aren't very interested in what *any* churches have to offer. When they move to a new city they may visit a nearby congregation to see what it is like, but they feel no compelling urge to get involved. They haven't left. They just aren't coming.[15]

For the most part, we have inoculated our children against the techniques conservative denominations use to great advantage among their own constituencies. The children of mainline church members know that the church is not the only source of truth. They are wary of authority and positively cringe at moralism and judgmental attitudes. Traditionally, the church was able to rely on its status as the keeper of spiritual truth and the susceptibility of its members to motivation because of guilt. This is true no more; and particularly for mainline churches outside the deep South.

Mainline churches are designed to decline, not by driving people away, but by failing to be useful, relevant, or interesting. A legitimate question to ask is "what are they for?" To reiterate the question posed earlier, if Disney makes people happy and McDonald's makes hamburgers, what does the mainline church make?

If we want different results, we must redesign the system so that declining membership is not what we produce. This does not mean that our focus should be on membership growth, of course. Growth is a byproduct of institutional health and not our primary objective.

---

14. Becoming less white by recruiting and establishing churches among persons of color (a growing population) is a systemic solution, although one that a cynic would call self-serving.

15. Reginald Wayne Bibby, *Fragmented Gods: The Poverty and Potential of Religion in Canada* (Toronto: Irwin, 1987).

A SYSTEMS MODEL

Any organism or organization can be thought of as a simple throughput system. Things are taken into the system, something happens to the things in the system, and something is produced by the system. The input, the transformational processes within the organism, and its products depend on the nature of the system.

It's easy to think about our bodies as systems. We take in oxygen and food. These inputs are transformed within our bodies. As a result of the transformational process, energy is released for work and some of the raw material becomes part of our bodies. We also produce a certain amount of byproducts in the form of waste. McDonald's operates as a system. Food and paper materials are taken in, transformed into hamburgers, fries, and pies by employees; these products are then put in bags and boxes and these products are then sold. Disneyland is a system that attempts to transform stressed people into happy people. But what about the church? What are its inputs? What changes take place within it? And what are its products and byproducts?

The products of a church depend on the nature of its inputs (resources) and the transformational process that occurs within the system. Some organizations only produce things they use themselves. Products in the form of friendships, a congenial social environment, networking opportunities, and so forth result from the interaction of people within the group. A regular input of additional people isn't required and the church may see little need for a visible output in terms of changed lives or service to the community. The church can become a relatively closed system that uses most of its energy simply to maintain its existence and keep its membership happy. It exists to satisfy people, not to change them; to meet their "felt needs," not to deal with the causes of their discomfort.

Churches that operate as social clubs or families are designed to produce community and little else. If we want different results we have to redesign the system. It is not a matter of getting rid of what we don't want or fixing what seems to be broken. Analyzing problems will not give us solutions. Instead, we should focus on finding "solution structures"—descriptions of what we want to happen as defined by our purpose.[16]

---

16. Bela H. Banathy, *Designing Social Systems in a Changing World* (New York: Plenum Press, 1996), 20, 56.

Our problems cry out for action and the natural reaction is to respond to the problems directly, rather than pursuing a systemic redesign. Before rushing in to fix a problem, we should remember two things: 1) "the harder you push, the harder the system pushes back"; and 2) "immediate benefits provided by a quick fix will be followed by long-term disbenefits."[17] Everything in a system is related to everything else, so being proactive in one area may only destabilize the system and cause even worse problems to develop—problems that seem unrelated to the original problem and our efforts to solve it.

Churches and denominational agencies tend to think programmatically rather than systemically. We evaluate the success of each area of ministry separately and think of them as if they were zero sum games. We ask, "are our evangelism efforts effective?" and "are we doing enough social justice?" Energy, effort, and funds for one area of ministry must mean less for another. This zero sum aspect of programmatic thinking was brought home to me quite vividly when I was criticized for talking about spirituality and the need for congregational renewal. One agency leader said that my efforts were racist. Another said that I was ignoring our social justice commitments. Why were my activities presumed to be racist and anti-justice? Tom Dipko, then head of the United Church Board for Homeland Ministries, explained it to me: A focus on worship, spirituality, and congregational renewal was seen as taking money and energy away from social action. It was perceived as a zero-sum game.

From a programmatic perspective, attention directed at one program will indeed take it away from another, but from a systemic perspective, attention directed at one area of ministry may actually enhance another. Several authors, including Ezra Earl Jones, Bill Easum, and Tom Bandy, have elaborated a useful systemic model of the church which is composed of three "flows": inviting, growing, and sending. These flows are all related to one another and all support one another. The inviting, the growing, and the sending are not disconnected programs to be resourced; they are systemic flows to be enhanced. According to Ezra Earl Jones, "in the church, the essential flow [of the system] involves people being invited and received into the church, transformed at the core of their being as they are related to

---

17. Peter M. Senge, *The Fifth Discipline: The Art and Practice of the Learning Organization* (New York: Currency/Doubleday, 1990), 58–60.

God and nurtured in the faith, and then sent out to live as disciples of the risen Christ."[18]

Inviting ➜ [Transformation] ➜ Sending

According to this systemic model, the sending process results from transformation. Persons of faith who have been transformed through the ministries of the church are sent out to live as disciples in the world. They share their gifts with others—their families, friends, community, and society. They are given permission to start ministries, to do ministry, and as Easum and Bandy put it "to take responsibility for the [child] of God they have become, nurturing life in healthy ways."[19]

The sending out to live as disciples (which may include organized efforts as well as individual acts) clearly involves social justice. Church members will be sent out to do what their faith implies. From a systemic perspective, however, the sending is not a matter of telling members what injustices they should oppose and expecting them to act. It also is not a matter of encouraging members to participate in existing causes. The energy and motivation to do any form of ministry must come from a prior faith commitment that we cannot assume already exists. Just because local church clergy or denominational staff may devote their lives to worthy causes such as freeing political prisoners and combating racial stereotyping doesn't mean that the people at First Presbyterian Church will care enough about these issues or any other justice issues to do anything about them.

The transformational process is logically prior to the sending process.[20] People cannot be sent out to live as disciples until they start becoming disciples. As they experience the transforming presence of God, understand

---

18. Jones, "The United Methodist Church," 17. Also see James D. Anderson and Ezra Earl Jones, *The Management of Ministry* (San Francisco: Harper & Row, 1978), 113. Norman Shawchuck and Roger Heuser add a helpful feedback loop to the systems model, which gives the organization "information about the congregation's state of health." See *Leading the Congregation: Caring for Yourself while Serving Others* (Nashville, Tenn.: Abingdon Press, 1993), 209.

19. William M. Easum and Thomas G. Bandy, *Growing Spiritual Redwoods* (Nashville, Tenn.: Abingdon, 1997), 208.

20. In a properly operating system where ministries are connected rather than isolated, involvement in social justice activities will aid in the process of personal transformation. It is a cycle, not a causal sequence.

Christ's mission, learn to forget self, and recognize the reality of God's Realm, people begin to see the world from a different perspective. As people of faith who are open to the truth—"no matter what the consequences, no matter where it leads you"—they may see the necessity for radical and counter-cultural ministries.[21] They will not need the motivation of guilt to pursue faithful action. But without this personal change, growth, and transformation, most North American church members will switch their brains into "pause" mode when their ministers begin talking about dismantling injustice. They will see their pastor's discourse in this area as something ministers do that can be safely ignored.

This is not to say that all members lack the driving interest in sending in the form of social justice ministry. Indeed, some members may have joined your church because of the commitment of your denomination to such ministry. Nevertheless, most church members will not share such a concern, nor do they have a latent interest that can be stimulated by exhortation on the subject.

Inviting also is intrinsically connected to transformation. It would be easy to read "inviting" as "evangelism" and see this process as a program to be resourced. From a program perspective, a problem with outreach must be fixed by enhancing evangelism efforts. We buy bigger ads, run television spots, preach about reaching the lost, hold evangelism-training seminars, organize evangelism committees, or set goals for new members and expect the church to achieve them. None of this is likely to help much, however, because new people will only disrupt the flow of the system—they are a lot of trouble; and they won't be accepted anyway. Furthermore, if church members have not grown in their faith, how can they share with it others?

From a systemic perspective, lack of outreach or evangelism implies that the system is not set up to accept people (as input) in order to produce disciples (as output). The only input is what current members bring to the system and the only output is what benefit these members receive through their participation. In many plateaued and declining churches, the benefits that members receive do not seem very substantial. However, it is *their church*.

---

21. Anthony de Mello, *Awareness: A de Mello Spirituality Conference in His Own Words*, ed. J. Francis Stroud (New York: Image Books/Doubleday, 1990), 18. I also like the way Rosemary Ruether puts it, "The church stands as the eschatological community over against the world not to de-create the world but to re-create it," as quoted in "Rosemary Ruether and Thomas Merton on Creation and Salvation," *The Christian Century* (22–29 March 1995): 331.

Their friends attend it with them, and it satisfies their need for community and their responsibility for weekly church attendance. To get anything out of such a church, one must be a long-term, core member.

The only effective outreach programs I have ever seen are means of channeling enthusiasm that was already there. The transformational process naturally produces "heat." Members are excited about what is happening to them and in their church. They want to invite people so others can see it and experience it for themselves. They also may believe that the type of transformation that reordered their lives is the only hope for hurting people and a suffering world. Organized evangelism or outreach efforts can help snuff the enthusiasm out of people's interest in inviting if it is seen as Christian responsibility or an end in itself. What a church can do is provide the resources members need to invite others more effectively. In all aspects of inviting or sending (evangelism, effective social action, and ethical living) acting in a Christ-like manner is "based on what God has given and makes possible, not on some perception of what God [or the church] demands."[22]

I have diagrammed the inviting, transforming, and sending processes as separate (see diagram on page 30), but they should not be seen as analytically distinct. The interconnectedness of the processes is not a minor point and thinking about both the inviting and the sending as contributing to personal transformation may also help keep us from lapsing back into a programmatic mindset. The openness that inviting assumes allows more growth to occur, and as we go out to minister we settle and establish our transforming nature. All of the processes have the same central purpose: forming a vessel with the capacity for transformation. The result of the transformational system (changed lives) is the product of the church. Disney makes people happy, we make people of faith who live like natives in God's Realm.

FROM VICIOUS TO VIRTUOUS CYCLES

Systems thinking can be complex, particularly when it comes to figuring out the real source of our problems. Since we know that problems in one area are probably caused by glitches elsewhere in the cycle, it may be diffi-

---

22. Victor Paul Furnish, "Can Ethics Be Christian?" *The Christian Century* (26 October 1994): 992. The bracketed "or the church" is added.

cult to properly diagnose what is really wrong with the system. Luckily, such diagnostic work usually isn't essential. Our focus should be on systemic solutions, rather than correcting specific glitches in the existing operation. We reset the system by focusing on our purpose and enhancing the flow of the processes that allow that purpose to be fulfilled. Doing so is the mission of a congregation.

Focusing on problems creates a vicious cycle in which efforts in one area cause new problems in another area. Efforts to fix subsequent problems cause additional imbalances in the system. It is a vicious cycle of action and reaction that typically results in an organization that is obsessed with control. And in organizations where the means of control are inadequate (particularly in voluntary organizations like the church), efforts at control lead to politically motivated behavior and interpersonal conflict. Each action makes things worse. Such is the nature of a vicious cycle.

In a *virtuous cycle*, each change makes things better instead of making things worse. In *The Fifth Discipline*, Peter Senge describes the effect of having a good product. Enhancing the product leads to satisfied customers. Having satisfied customers leads to positive word of mouth. Positive word of mouth leads to more sales. More sales of a good product leads to more satisfied customers. And so on. It is a virtuous cycle where enhancements in one area produce positive results in another.[23]

It is possible to pump up sales through advertising or by cutting prices. But if the product is bad, customers will not be satisfied, leading to negative word of mouth and, eventually, to lower sales. If we focus only on the problem as a matter of sales, however, when sales decline we will have to blame our efforts in this area and spend even more money on advertising (or fire the marketing manager). We also may try to compensate for having a bad product by focusing on customer satisfaction. A business might employ a large force of service consultants or a problem-solving hot line to increase customer satisfaction—even while maintaining a mediocre product. One would think that creating a better product would be the obvious solution to corporate problems, but when the problem is seen as a lack of sales, a more direct solution would seem to be in marketing, not product development. Businesses, like churches, tend to assume that they have a good product and are dismayed that people don't seem to want it.

---

23. Senge, *The Fifth Discipline*, 81.

When people analyze the product of the church these days, they tend to do so in terms of the attractiveness of the worship service. It should be interesting and exciting; it should use television monitors, LCD projectors, holographic replicators, state-of-the-art amplified surround sound, sound mixers, synthesizers, and computer feedback stations for worshipers.[24] Efforts to enhance the appeal of worship services only constitutes advertising in disguise. So-called "seeker services" are ways of drawing people in and showing them that the church really isn't so bad—it's just like going to a concert and motivational lecture rolled in to one.

The product of the church is changed lives, not quality worship. Thus, enhancing worship is only relevant in terms of the transformational effect it has on the people who attend. It should not be used as advertising, because doing so creates a vicious cycle of providing better and better worship events in order to attract people who are turned off by the church.[25] By attracting many seekers to worship, but only drawing a few into the transformational activities of the church, seeker-sensitive churches run the risk of goal displacement, through which secondary purposes become primary.

What the church offers is a supportive community of faith where people can grow spiritually and learn to live authentically. The entire system that is the church should support this central purpose—especially its worship services. If people are growing, being transformed, then a church can say it has a quality product. If a church is not yet there, church leaders should begin moving in that direction by setting up reinforcing processes that will result in a virtuous cycle.

Once a church begins to concentrate on its primary business rather than on attracting an audience, working a program, or satisfying its members, the decisions required for continued improvement should be obvious. Once in place and producing products for which they were designed, systems tend to be self-organizing. That is, they do not need micromanagement. Let the system grow, and don't try to over-institutionalize it or constrain its evolution. Encourage, water, and fertilize its growth. Let it bloom, share in the harvest, prune it when necessary, and keep an eye out for bugs.

---

24. See Easum and Bandy, *Growing Spiritual Redwoods*, 71.

25. According to Robert Marrone, pastor of St. Peter Church in Cleveland, Ohio, what churches are doing is "trying to buoy up weak primary symbols with stronger secondary symbols" (personal interview, St. Peter Church, 27 Jan. 1999), Instead of emphasizing people, bread, wine, table, etc. we stress peripheral symbols. So, "when you do something big every week, then what you need to do to make a point has to be bigger and bigger."

Chapter four

A CONGREGATIONAL TYPOLOGY

WHY INTRODUCE A NEW TYPOLOGY for understanding congregations? Don't good ones already exist that church leaders find useful for understanding the diversity of church organization and mission?[1] Why add another? There are two reasons. First, this book presents a different perspective on church transformation and previous models do not capture what I am trying to say. Second, this new model can be diagrammed in dynamic form (in chap. 5), and as the saying goes, "a picture is worth a thousand words." I won't have to write as much explanation and you won't have to read it. This model is not better than any previous one, but it does do something different than other models: It shows why some strategies for change work and others do not.

As with all typologies, the types themselves are not real. Churches are real. Types are concepts that reduce the incarnational complexity of real churches to a set of key characteristics. Is it easy to see how your church fits in one type better than in another? Does seeing the distinction between types help you understand churches better? If the answer to both questions is yes, we have a useful model. Even so, we need to resist the temptation to say my church is one of the types or another. It is not. Your congregation is unique.

THE CLUB OR CLAN

Since most churches are small and because most churches in traditionally Christian countries are more than twenty years old, congregations that fit the image of *club or clan* are numerous and widely distributed, at least within

---

1. Avery Dulles, *Models of the Church*, exp. ed. (Garden City, N.Y.: Image Books, 1987) is one of the best examples of a church typology. Also see David A. Roozen, William McKinney, and Jackson W. Carroll, *Varieties of Religious Presence: Mission in Public Life* (New York: The Pilgrim Press, 1984).

Protestant denominations. The church as club or clan is easily described and should be quite familiar.

This type of church is a relatively closed community of members who have been together for years. More often than not, authority is in the hands of a few laypersons and their extended families. The pastor may have some authority, but unless she has been there for a long time, the more typical role she plays is that of "clan priest" or "hired hand"—a religious functionary who is hired to preach, teach, marry, bury, and visit the sick and homebound.

Traditions are strong and intentional change is unlikely in clannish churches. When change does occur, it requires the approval of long-term members who form the heart and soul of the congregation. These realities are illustrated by the story of a United Church of Christ minister in western Pennsylvania who returned as pastor to the church of her childhood where all of her grandparents were buried in the church cemetery. She discovered upon arrival that the small congregation had very some odd financial practices, including multiple checking accounts. When the church secretary was asked why they managed their finances in such a strange way, the woman replied that she didn't know and that she hadn't been able to change a thing since she started paying the church's bills. She added, somewhat excitedly: "but you might be able to change them, because you are blood!" Becoming "blood" apparently takes several generations in this church, so the possibility of a pastor with no family connections changing anything was very unlikely.

A key defining characteristic of the church as club or clan is *community*. Members know one another well and meet together primarily because of the character of the group, whether they profess to enjoy being there or not. They belong to the church in the same way that you and I belong to our extended families. So even though they may dislike a few of the members and tolerate a pushy preacher, they will attend because it is *their church*.

Some churches of this type are warm, hospitable places that make newcomers welcome. Others are full of festering wounds, remembered slights, and struggles for control. Most churches fall somewhere in between. Because of their cohesive nature, it should be no surprise that the church as club or clan tends to be somewhat smaller than the average congregation in North America.[2] As organizations become larger, problems of scale reduce the sense of being a single social group where everyone knows one another well.

A second key defining characteristic of the church as club or clan is culture. *All* churches are cultural groups in that they develop accepted, taken-for-granted patterns of perception and discrimination—social conventions with a sense of "oughtness" about them. However, to the extent that a church's operative purpose is more about maintaining community than about getting things done, the stronger will be its sense of cultural distinctiveness.

Culture should not be thought of as a "thing" or an entity. It has no elements to be identified. Culture is a process, a commonality of perception that conditions people to see things in similar ways. Culture colors our thinking in much the same way that Easter eggs are colored by being immersed in a glass of dye. The longer we remain within a distinctive subculture, the more deeply and obviously we are colored by it. For persons who have spent a lot of time in a single, inward-looking church, the conditioning effect may be strong. That congregation forms their image of a good church and the people who make up that congregation define for them what church members should be like.

Several years ago Penny Marler, associate professor of religion at Samford University, and I conducted a research project on the unchurched, funded by the Lilly Endowment. As part of this project, we interviewed unchurched persons around the country and happened to talk to a middle-aged man in Phoenix, Arizona, who identified strongly with the Church of Christ. This man, whom I will call John, almost never attends church despite having very conservative religious views and a judgmental attitude toward "liberal churches" and "lost people" in his community. Why doesn't John go to church? He had tried over the years to get involved in several Church of Christ congregations (other denominations were out of the question), but he cannot find one like his home church in Yuma. For John, no other church felt right or did things like they did them in Yuma. So he only attends church when he returns home.

---

2. See Kenneth Pargament, William Silverman, Steven Johnson, Ruben Echemendia, and Susan Snyder, "The Psychosocial Climate of Religious Congregations," *American Journal of Community Psychology* 11, no. 4 (1983): 375. Also see Arlin J. Rothauge, *Sizing up a Congregation for New Member Ministry* (New York: Episcopal Church Center, n.d.).

Churches with a strong community life and an even stronger sense of "the way things ought to be done" are not limited to conservative denominations. Despite what Dean Kelly said about strictness and conservatism in *Why Conservative Churches Are Growing*, many liberal mainline churches also have a lot of rules which "must be obeyed." Their rules are not specifically about personal morality—drinking, smoking, fornicating, doing drugs, and the like—but they are rules about behavior. They may be about where one sits, what one says in business meetings, what one wears, but mostly they take the form of subtle rules which guide communication. What is it safe to talk about? *How* do people talk to each other? Is it no-nonsense, formal, folksy, task-oriented, playful, relaxed, courteous, or emotional? What are the unspoken assumptions that everyone knows but are too obvious to mention?

We often forget that people attach different meanings to the same words. People who don't know the code (particularly new church members) are at a great disadvantage and sometimes it seems like long-term members are trying to catch them making mistakes. Teaching newcomers by pointing out their mistakes is the method we use to communicate cultural assumptions, but it also is a form of group initiation. The stronger the sense of group cohesion, the more likely new members will receive messages which say, "you are different and not yet one of us."[3]

A sense of community is not a bad thing, of course. People want and expect any group to which they belong to be friendly and characterized by close personal relationships. Even in the business world, the best places to work in terms of employee satisfaction are said to feel like a family. Churches, even more than businesses, must have a strong sense of community. A common culture and identity helps bind people together.[4]

The primary problem with the church-as-club is not its sense of community, but the sense that community is its only reason for being. People expect to find friends when they join a church, but new social relationships are not the primary reason most people look for a church—particularly those who have been outside the church for a long time.

Despite the individualism that seems so prevalent in Western society, many opportunities exist for social involvement. Most of these opportunities—whether they are clubs, interest groups, classes, or simply fluid groups

---

3. Lee G. Bolman and Terrance E. Deal, *Reframing Organizations: Artistry, Choice, and Leadership* (San Francisco: Jossey-Bass, 1991), 248.

4. Mary Lynn Pulley, "Leading Resilient Organizations," *Leadership in Action* 17, no. 4 (1997): 3.

of friends or couples who do things together—feel much less demanding than the average church. Churches are often cliquish and communicate a sense of moralism and judgment about both behavior and ideas. Large numbers of unchurched North Americans say: "I don't need the church in order to find friends or to fill my social calendar."

What unchurched people are looking for is the same thing that everyone expects the church to be: a religious organization. It should look different, it should feel different, and it should sound different, because unlike every other organization in society its specialty is religion (rather than something else—group fun, golf, scuba diving, bowling, good books, etc.). After interviewing hundreds of people in the United States and Canada who don't go to church, I have concluded that the predominant view of the church is this: It is a not particularly enjoyable social group with a restricted view of morality and spirituality. Unchurched North Americans don't feel they need the church for social involvement; they don't think the church has a monopoly on truth; and they don't think the church would help them very much in their relationship with God.

The church as club or clan fills its religious calendar in the same way as other churches, but its worship, Christian education, and other rituals and programs are clearly secondary to the relationships members have with each other. It is easy for churches to devolve into clubs or community centers over time as they lose their focus and become places where people meet their friends, listen to a sermon, and engage in the necessary organizational activity to keep the business running. As organizational experts Lee Bolman and Terrance Deal note, "Groups often get lost."[5] They lose track of their purpose, their reason for being. People are there to be satisfied, not transformed. There is little inviting and even less sending.

The church as club or clan is resilient because most of its energy is directed toward satisfying current members. Furthermore, the strong sense of connection that members develop over time precludes much dropping out. It is much less a matter of formal membership than informal network formation. As the bad habits that reinforce its club-like nature become the deep ruts of unthinking routine, the church will be unaware of what it has become. So even though churches of this type may survive for many years, few new people will be attracted to them. And if people do try to join for

---

5. Bolman and Deal, *Reframing Organizations*, 150.

whatever reason, they may find it difficult to be fully accepted—unless they are "blood."

THE CHARISMATIC-LEADER-AND-FOLLOWERS

Some churches seem less like cohesive communities than like followers who cluster around a charismatic leader. Churches of this type are not very numerous, but sometimes they are quite visible. What may come to mind are television preachers and their "congregations" of followers. Without their preacher, no church would exist, or at least not one that was as large with as much money to be spent on so many ministries. Not content with the people they can draw to their congregation physically, they also attract followers via local television, cable, satellite, and direct mail.

The church as *charismatic-leader-and-followers* often grows very rapidly as the leader's preaching ability or sheer magnetic nature of his presence draws people in. Many struggling churches hope to find a charismatic preacher who will bring in more people and save them from their current membership decline and financial woes. Churches with a history of this sort of leadership—particularly large downtown churches—may find it necessary to replace one charismatic leader with another lest they begin to experience the same troubles as churches around them.

Change of leadership always provokes a crisis when the primary source of authority is charisma—as the über sociologist Max Weber pointed out many years ago. If the church is more of an audience for the leader than a group with a strong sense of belonging, what happens when a charismatic leader resigns, dies, or falls from grace in the manner of Jimmie Swaggart? What happens when the movement stops growing and it becomes obvious that the leader's vision will not be realized? Severe decline is usually the answer to all these questions unless there is a concerted effort to restructure the followers into an organized *group* and redirect enthusiasm away from the *person* of the leader toward his or her message. Even so, there are many examples where the transition did not take place. Jimmie Swaggart and Oral Robert's ministries are shadows of what they once were. Rex Humbard's Cathedral of Tomorrow was sold to Ernest Angley, and there are many other examples of spent charisma.

Obviously, there are also less extreme examples of this phenomenon. For instance, some churches of this type seem less like movements than collections of devotees clustered around their gurus. In such cases, there is no effort to become the greatest church in the city. Instead, members create a cult-like group of adoring followers. Not restricted to churches, this phenomenon also can be observed on college campuses, seminaries, and other settings that cultivate hero worship.

Many African American congregations fit the charismatic-leader-and-followers type because of the very dominant role played by the pastor in the black church. In most black churches, the pastor is expected to be the final authority and receives all sorts of respect, adulation, and gifts—to such an extent that white pastors express both surprise and a certain amount of envy when they find out what they are missing. Also, many black churches were actually organized by their senior minister. This reinforces his authority: he was the original member of the church and has both senior elder status and the office of pastor. Dynamic preaching is held in high regard in the African American community. It is expected, so a black preacher who lacks personal charisma and the ability to preach will not be successful. All of these factors reinforce the authority of the pastor in the African American church and result in a congregational structure that often is dominated by one individual. To the extent that this dominance results in a church that is more a leader and followers than a strong congregation, the church fits the type I am describing in this section.

A church only fits the charismatic-leader-and-followers type if the pastor really is the leader of the church and not just a dynamic preaching functionary who fills pews but does not have true authority over his or her congregation. The true charismatic leader controls the church and has final authority. The members trust their pastor implicitly and will do what she asks. Sometimes a preaching functionary may be able to mobilize his audience into a group of followers and thus into a base of power. More often, however, a dynamic minister might think he is the real leader of the church, but in fact he is only a well paid hired hand for the true owners.

In other situations, a pastor may have a great deal of power but not be a charismatic leader. Such churches vest great authority in the *office* of pastor or priest. It is not the person who has the authority, but the *position*. Churches of this type do not fit the charismatic leader and follower model of congregation.

New churches, of all varieties, often retain a charismatic-leader-and-followers orientation as long as the organizing minister is pastor of the church. The organizing minister may gather people who are drawn more to her than to the excitement of starting a new congregation. Finding pastors with magnetic personalities and a gift for persuasion is a good way to jump-start a new church. As with most things, however, the easy way is not the best way. Starting a church in this manner creates dependency, retards the formation of community, and provokes a crisis when the organizing pastor leaves the church.

Leadership is essential for churches, and the ability to communicate a message is very important for making worship a time of personal transformation. Problems develop when a pastor with personal charisma allows church members to turn into a group of followers rather than to become a community.

THE COMPANY OR CORPORATION

The second largest group of churches in North America, after the church as clan or club, can be called the church as *company or corporation*.[6] There are some very fine and selfless congregations in this category and many do a lot of good. They are organized to do what they intend to do and set out to perform their appointed tasks.

This type of church resembles a company or corporation in that it is organized to produce a predefined product. The church as company or corporation understands what a good church should be doing and puts in place the proper programs to ensure that the right types of ministry occur. The results of these programmatic ministries can then be measured: X number of masses were held, Y number of perfect attendance badges were awarded, Z number of baptisms were recorded. They may even go beyond raw numbers to ratios and rates, giving more importance to one part of the equation than to another (e.g. to adult converts rather than to adult transfers).

For instance, Southern Baptist churches traditionally place a great deal of importance on Sunday school, seeing it as more than just Christian education. In order to make Sunday school function as a setting for evangelism, denominational guidelines suggest that a concerted effort should be made to enroll as many people as possible—including people who are not members of the church. A good church will have a high Sunday school to church member ratio. Presumably, evangelism *and* Christian education will be the result.

---

6. Another possible name is the "program church."

Roman Catholic parishes tend to count ritual observances rather than the persons actually participating in them. How many masses were performed; how many weddings, funerals, and baptisms were held? Proper rituals equal effectiveness in doing the work of the church and making good Catholics.

But what happens when the numbers don't look so good anymore? Then we ignore the numbers and put even more trust in the ability of the organization to get the job done.

The church as company or corporation is program-oriented, and the programs of the church are defined by their missional objectives. The problem is that setting up the proper structure, working the proper program, and measuring things that are presumably related to the effectiveness of the program tend to become ends in themselves, rather than ways to actualize the purpose of the church. It is not that we are just going through the motions, it is that the motions become more important than the reasons we are doing them. These motions (programs) can even become the products of the church, to which people are attracted, thus leading to a false sense that goals are being accomplished.

Churches are not businesses that produce specific, easily measured products (people or programs). As noted in chapters 2 and 3, the goals of a church are diffuse and hard to measure. Churches should be *religious* organizations, communities that change lives and change the world. The nature of these hoped-for changes is open-ended and cannot be set beforehand. If the change is happening, we will know it, but it is awfully hard to measure our outcomes, or at least to express them in the form of tangible corporate goals.

Corporations and other for-profit businesses provide the organizational models for our churches despite the fact that the goals of the former are very different from the goals of the latter. From a corporate perspective, churches should have clearly defined goals and rationally designed programs to achieve those goals. When goals are ambiguous, multiple, and diffuse, however, it is extremely difficult to design mechanisms that result in the desired end state. The technology is not there; doing this action will not necessarily cause that change. Nor is the command structure in place to get the job done; churches rely almost exclusively on informal networks.[7]

---

7. Bolman and Deal, *Reframing Organizations*, 46, 244, 245.

Trying to run a church using a rational, goal-directed model may result in some good things being done. Usually, however, churches built on this model become bureaucratic institutions where the true goal is to keep the organization running and the numbers up.

THE INCARNATIONAL COMMUNITY

> As geese fly in flocks and seeds become trees,
> so we grow in communities of faith
> continually becoming what God already sees

I offer this proverb as a reminder to be what we already are and to do what churches do. We should not forget that we are churches rather than social clubs, and we should not emulate corporations by trying to be successful and efficient in our efforts to create disciples. Our central goal is to be the church, naturally and without striving for optimal effectiveness in reaching the world for Christ.

The church as *incarnational community* seeks to embody Christ's mission by proclaiming that the Realm of God is here—and by *living in it*. We are to incarnate, enflesh, and embody Christ and Christ's message. To do this, we must grow as his disciples, and in order to grow we must be open to change, to transformation.

Describing the church as incarnational community is more difficult than defining what it is not.[8] It's like trying to describe "happiness" or "God." Anthony de Mello says you can only hint at it: "One cannot say anything about happiness. Happiness cannot be defined. What can be defined is misery. Drop unhappiness and you will know . . . But you'll know only when you get there."[9]

Obviously, the incarnational community is not the other three types, yet it is also not their antithesis and, in fact, has things in common with all three. The incarnational community is a community. Churches should have a full and rich group life. Members know and love each other; they also

---

8. The familiar analogy of what a sculptor does may be apt here. He chips away everything that doesn't look like what he is carving. In order to find the incarnational community, we clear away everything that doesn't look like it.

9. Anthony de Mello, *Awareness: A de Mello Spirituality Conference in His Own Words*, ed. J. Francis Stroud (New York: Doubleday/Image Books, 1990), 98.

squabble and fight from time to time. They are families of faith. So the church as incarnational community shares some common features with the church as club or clan.

The incarnational community is not directionless. It assumes creative activity—bringing new things into being. Its purpose is not to achieve some predetermined goal, however. It is not trying to accumulate members or reach some desired (ideal) end point. Its purpose, instead, is to act in a direct resolute way in keeping with its nature. Just as a doctor should mend wounds and a farmer should plant crops, so a church should grow persons of faith. Being the church presumes purposeful action and direction, so the church as incarnational community shares some things in common with the church as company or corporation. There is something to be grown or produced, transformed and sent. Doing so is the mission of the church.

Keeping the church oriented in a direction consistent with its mission requires leadership. Thus the church as incarnational community shares some things in common with the church as charismatic-leader-and-followers. Community, resolute action, and leadership each are important aspects of any church. It should be clear, however, that an imbalance in any one of the three directions could subvert the purpose of the church. Essentially, we know something is wrong when we have too much of anything: Community, leadership or purposeful action.

The nature of God's Realm is not what we expect it to be, nor does it conform to our preconceived notions of how it should be run. It is a place of transformation. And what is transformation? It is a "magical" process whereby ingredients are combined to make something new, something quite different from a simple mixture of those ingredients. When yeast is added to flour and water, the dough changes and begins to rise; when a scientist mixes ingredients and adds a catalyst a chemical reaction occurs. "Behold, I begin a new thing, now it shall spring forth" (Isa. 43:19 [DARBY]).

As churches, we supply the baking pan and the ingredients for change. We put them together and allow God to work—to produce the reaction that transforms the ingredients (us) into something new. Just as the shape and texture of the bread we bake may vary according to the type of flour, the humidity, the altitude, the amount of kneading, the heat of the oven, and many other factors, so the outcome of our transformation cannot be predetermined. The different gifts members bring to the mixture are after all much more complex than those that might go into a loaf of bread or a cake. There is no telling what new thing a church will bake.

The point is that we cannot control the direction of God's transformation and we should not want to try. Trusting God and being open to change allows disparate people to bring their own unique gifts and characteristics to the process. People are treated as "deep wells" from which they and the church can draw refreshing new things.[10] The supply is never diminished.

The uncontrollable aspect of transformation may seem a bit scary and something to be avoided. We tend, usually, to err on the side of control, so the situation doesn't get out of hand. Tight control is an aspect of structurally oriented businesses and works against the very things that symbolically oriented voluntary organizations want to accomplish. For churches and other organizations that are concerned with changing people, the organizational processes they use are more important for what they *express* than for what they *produce*.[11] In other words the focus can never be on the production, but always on the process. The nature of the results cannot be predetermined, but we can be sure that great results will be produced if due attention is given to the process.

In the case of the church, the process results in changed lives, and as with any transformative, catalytic reaction, it also produces a certain amount of heat. Heat is excitement and enthusiasm about what has happened and what is happening in the church and in people's lives. For churches and other organizations with diffuse goals, the excitement, enthusiasm, and motivation are much more important than correct decisions or proper planning. The church is a growing thing, and it is the members who supply the raw materials for that growth. Decisions and plans are only our efforts to channel the growth of the organism. Even if we make a mistake in our efforts to direct its growth, our "tree" will continue to thrive and compensate for our mistakes—because it is alive.

When churches and church members are transformed (and this is a *continual* process, much like photosynthesis), they will do ministry in unexpected ways. They will "allow their natures to select their choices."[12] They will develop new ministries about which they are excited. They will inno-

---

10. This imagery was suggested in a conversation with Bill Green at the national offices of The United Church of Christ in Cleveland, Ohio. It was drawn from an article by William Kahn, "To Be Fully There," *Human Relations* 45, no. 4 (1992): 321–49.

11. Bolman and Deal, *Reframing Organizations*, 61.

12. Stanley M. Herman, *The Tao at Work: On Leading and Following* (San Francisco: Jossey-Bass, 1994), 60.

vate rather than imitate, and efforts to drum up excitement about a new ministry will not be required. If people feel passionately about something, they will not view doing it as a chore or as their duty to the church; they will see it as their personal mission.

The church as incarnational community will not do just a few things well; it will become a setting for transformation and will empower its members to pursue a multitude of ministries, as long as those ministries are consistent with the unfolding identity of the church. This openness and lack of control will lead to problems, of course, but as long as problems are expected they will not catch the church by surprise. Problems may come to be seen not as problems, but as changes in the context of ministry—as new ingredients—added to the continuing process of transformation.

The church as incarnational community will never feel that it has arrived. Indeed, it may think that it has more in common with one of the other three types. If we think we have never seen churches like this, we are wrong. They are all around us. They are congregations where people worship God, love one another, and seek to be real rather than an impossible ideal.

Chapter five

A DYNAMIC MODEL

A NEW CONGREGATIONAL TYPOLOGY was outlined in the previous chapter. Some churches forget why they exist and devolve into congenial, but directionless, social groups. I call such churches *clubs or clans*. Other churches fall under the control of a charismatic leader. They succeed or fail depending on the ability of one person to attract followers. This is the *charismatic-leader-and-followers* church. A third type of church, which I call the *company or corporation*, is goal-directed and task-oriented. It has put in place a structure and programs designed to accomplish its mission. The final type, the *incarnational community*, has a strong sense of community, but also wants to transform people—to liberate them into God's Realm. Its leaders provide direction but do not control the congregation. It has structure and programs but is more concerned about their character than about what they accomplish. The bottom line for the incarnational community is the answer to this question: Is the church being formed and does it have the capacity to transform individual lives?

In this chapter the typology introduced in the previous chapter is transformed into a dynamic model. The four types are placed into four cells of a two-by-two grid. As can be seen in figure 1, the grid is defined by crosscutting dimensions. Subsequent figures (2–5) show possible (and impossible) directions for change within the grid.

The defining dimension at the top of the grid refers to the group's goals. Are they diffuse, intangible goals or specific, tangible goals?

GOALS: SPECIFIC OR DIFFUSE?

An organization's goals or desired outcomes can be either specific, tangible, and easy to measure or diffuse, intangible, and hard to measure. The Ford Motor Company produces automobiles; Microsoft produces software; farms produce crops; consulting firms produce recommendations and advice. In

Figure I

A NEW MODEL FOR

CONGREGATIONAL ANALYSIS

	DIFFUSE (INTANGIBLE) GOALS	SPECIFIC (TANGIBLE) GOALS
PURPOSE IN PLACE (CHANGE PEOPLE)	**INCARNATIONAL COMMUNITY** *A Culture of Transformation* • Open-ended, permission-giving • Embodies its purpose • Nurtures and grows • Transforms one another • Visual image: Aspen grove	**COMPANY OR CORPORATION** *An Organization with a Plan* • Goal-directed, outcome-oriented • Works its program • Measures its ministry • Molds its members • Visual image: Factory
PURPOSE DISPLACED (SATISFY PEOPLE)	**CLUB OR CLAN** *A Congenial Community* • Tradition-bound, inward-looking • Owner-occupied • Like a family, hard to join • Satisfies each other • Visual image: Recliner	**CHARISMATIC LEADER AND FOLLOWERS** *A Movement under Command* • Vision-directed, often misaimed • Follows its leader • Boom or bust • Satisfies its leader • Visual image: Guided missile

each case it is easy to identify the product that the company produces through its transformational processes. Inputs are transformed into tangible outputs—which business schools sometimes call *widgets*. These widgets (products and services) are then sold to people outside the firm in exchange for resources that keep the company going.

Churches are not widget-producing businesses. Congregations have diffuse desired outcomes that are difficult to grasp and even harder to measure. The outcome is a state of being that has intrinsic rather than instrumental value. We are not alone in this. Colleges, universities, hospitals, legislatures, government agencies, charities, and mental health organizations share the same sort of vexing goals. What are the outcomes? What does an educated student look like? What is the nature of mental health? What is a good community? What is artistic appreciation? What is a person of faith and how can we know if one is produced?

Organizations that have diffuse goals also have uncertain means to achieve them. It is never a matter of X causing Y. There is no linear cause-and-effect connection between activities and outcomes. As Lee Bolman and Terrance Deal note in *Reframing Organizations*, "In such organizations, most things are ambiguous. Who has power? What is success? Why was a decision made? What are the goals? The answers are often veiled in a fog of uncertainty."[1] Such is the nature of organizations with diffuse goals.

Even though one of the defining characteristics of non-profit organizations like the church is diffuse, intangible, difficult-to-measure goals, the North American need to accomplish something is so strong that churches try to act like something they are not. They develop clear, specific, tangible objectives in order to accomplish something great for God, their leader, or their trustees.

On the right side of the grid (fig. 1), both the company or corporation and the charismatic-leader-and-followers churches are concerned about getting specific, tangible things done. The company or corporation church (top right) wants to create the right programs, ministries, and worship services in order to effect change in its members and society. Through the operation of its structure and programs, people will learn things about the Bible and come to salvation in Christ. If the ideology of the church is somewhat different, people will learn about social justice and fight against op-

---

1. Lee Bolman and Terrance Deal, *Reframing Organizations: Artistry, Choice, and Leadership* (San Francisco: Jossey-Bass, 1991), 245, 272.

pression. Objectives are limited and fit well within a corporate planning model. The church understands that its purpose is to make disciples, but rather than trust the unpredictable process of transformation, the church as company or corporation seeks to mold and shape (form) people into a predetermined image (impossible ideal) of what good Christians should look like and how they should behave.

The church as charismatic-leader-and-followers (bottom right) also has specific tangible goals, but rather than flowing from communal purposes, its objectives and directions are defined by their leader. In order to "build a fire under them," in the words of Florida State coach Bobby Bowden, followers need simple, easily-grasped objectives. The leader provides the simplified statement of the problem, the sense of urgency about what must be done, a vision of what the results will be, and the plan to be followed. By obeying the leader's commands, victory will be assured and the vision will be realized. Or, if the leader is more of a guru than a commander, the objective may be to meet that leader's need for hero worship while at the same time satisfying the desire for meaning and direction among their followers.

On the left side of the model are the incarnational community and the club or clan churches. Both lack specific, easily-measured goals. What is the goal of a family? It might be to nurture the growth of one's children so that they will become successful, loving, morally-responsible persons. What is the goal of a social club? It might be to provide a setting for satisfying social relationships. Both "morally-responsible persons" and "satisfying social relationships" are difficult concepts to define and even more difficult to measure. They are diffuse, multifaceted things that, like a good meal, can be declared good only after they have been tasted. So the diffuse goal of the church as club or clan (lower left) is to be a congenial Christian community where supportive relationships exist and where involvement symbolizes commitment to God and good Christian values.

The church as incarnational community does not define its purposes in specific, tangible terms, nor does it confuse its structure and programs with its purpose. By understanding that the outcome of transformation cannot be controlled, such churches focus on becoming spiritual vessels with the capacity for transformation. They produce people who see life differently and act accordingly. The incarnational community allows ministries to emerge that fulfill the personal missions of each member. Evaluation and measurement are not directed at specific, tangible results, but at how the ministries/programs/worship services are conducted (quality, timing, response, "feel," etc.) and at how the experience contributes to the transformational process. According to Edward Fischer, "the *way* something is done is at the foundation of religious life. No activity is religious if it lowers life, and none is secular if it lifts life. How a thing is done is rock-bottom communication that goes beyond all words and turns an act into worship or into blasphemy."[2]

The quality of an action and its contribution to transformation are things not easily measured, nor are they very specific things. The church as incarnational community does not look at goals as goals. There is an outcome, of course, a product of transformation. But seen through "instrumental eyes," it may not look like success.[3] Incarnational communities are not trying to become *great* churches; they are satisfied with being *real* churches.

PURPOSE: IN PLACE OR DISPLACED?

The second dimension of the model, shown on the left side of figure 1, refers to purpose. Is purpose "in place" or "displaced"? Purpose, as I talk about it throughout this book, refers to the business of the church—its reason for being. Is the *operative* purpose to change people or to satisfy them? For the church, focusing on satisfying someone's needs (our own or our leader's) is evidence of a displaced purpose.

For both the incarnational community and the church as company or corporation, the structure, programs, and activities of the church are directed at accomplishing its mission. For churches that fit into these two cells, purpose is clearly in place. The objectives of the church are consistent with the desire to change people's lives.

The church as company or corporation might seem to be the best type of church in that churches of this variety understand their mission and put programs in place to reach specific, mission-related goals. Some "missional churches" are very effective at actually achieving their goals. With a single-minded focus on accomplishing tasks designed with the mission in mind,

---

2. Edward Fischer, *Everybody Steals from God: Communication as Worship* (Notre Dame, Ind.: Notre Dame University Press, 1977), 124.

3. In a personal comment to me on this section, Larry Peers wrote, "Embodying and witnessing to the 'Kingdom (Reign) of God' is not reducible to 'goals' or 'success' since the Crucifixion and other events seem like failure through instrumental eyes."

the church as company or corporation gets things done. A clear, selfless purpose is not their problem. It is one of their strengths. The problem, as discussed earlier, refers to the way purpose is translated into specific, tangible goals, thereby subverting the very purpose they were designed to fulfill.

A related problem, also mentioned previously, is the tendency to mistake an active program for success at achieving one's goals. Not all churches that fit the company or corporation type are successful organizations. Indeed, one of the most prevalent varieties of this type are large, non-growing, bureaucratic, Protestant churches that have programs, committees, and staff in place in each area that their denomination defines as appropriate. They have strong Christian education programs with a minister of education and a large educational wing. They have a minister of music, graded choirs, handbells, and ensembles. They have an active youth program, a singles ministry, softball teams, craft classes, a food pantry, senior adult trips, and Tae-bo. There is nothing wrong with any of these ministries and programs. It is just that maintaining a proper program tends to become the operative objective (rather than the means to reach the original objectives of the church). Successful organizations tend to relax and put faith in the procedures that got them where they are, forgetting that it was the energy channeled through their programs and not the programs themselves that led to their success.

Roman Catholic churches that have allowed their theological understanding of the efficacy of the sacraments to degrade the attention given to their rites are also prevalent in this category. Too often Catholic parishioners endure tedious homilies and masses that priests perform by rote. Members seem to ignore what is happening at the altar and end up worshiping God privately in their pews with the church only providing a place for them to do it. In both Protestant and Catholic churches, too much faith is placed on having the right actions occur.

The church as incarnational community also has its purpose in place. It does not try to construct or rationally plan the proper structure, however. Doing so secularizes what is built because it follows the logic of control rather than incarnation.[4] Instead, the incarnational community allows structure, programs, and ministries to develop and grow naturally as members express interest and excitement about ideas that give them energy and that

---

4. See Alexander Schmemann, *For the Life of the World: Sacrament and Orthodoxy* (Crestwood, N.Y.: St. Vladimir's Seminary Press, 1973), 125.

are consistent with the purpose of the church. Programs reinforce one another in such a way as to fulfill the overall purpose of the church. By focusing on how programs and other activities are done (rather than on getting them done or on their specific outcomes), the church as incarnational community does not allow its purpose to be undermined by derivative instrumental goals.

For both the church as club or clan and the church as charismatic-leader-and-followers (bottom half of the model), the purpose of the church is scarcely recognizable. "Displaced" may be too mild a term. Perhaps "replaced" would be better.

The church as club or clan has a purpose, but that purpose is essentially selfish and was not the reason the church was organized. It exists to serve and satisfy the needs of current members. It is content to be what it is, a close-knit community that worships together and tries to keep the pastor paid, the boiler fixed, and the fellowship suppers served. Religious purposes—being a place where people experience communion with God—are clearly secondary. Because the group calls itself a church it makes a reasonable stab at doing what a church is supposed to do; but maintaining a congenial community is its real purpose. The church as club or clan may feel like family to its members, and it can be as warm and friendly or as conflict-ridden and dysfunctional as any real family. For new residents to the area, however, the church as club or clan is hard to join. Some churches have a strong community life, but also make room for newcomers. They do not tend to be of this type, however. Rather, they are likely to be examples of the church as incarnational community (or churches becoming incarnational communities).

The church as charismatic-leader-and-followers also has a displaced purpose. Its purpose is to do whatever the leader decides it should do—to satisfy him or her. No matter how lofty that purpose is, to the extent that it originates with the charismatic leader, the church is pursuing the leader's selfish goals. Success is seen as a validation of the leader's vision and often goes to the leader's head. Criticisms of the leader's actions are taken personally. Everything is "about" the leader and it is impossible to remain a member of the group without being a follower. The only alternative roles are enemy and outsider.

To summarize, the church as incarnational community is *a culture of transformation* where members experience God and are transformed into persons of faith. We might visualize it as an Aspen Grove—which forms a single organism rather than individual trees. Like the aspen grove, the church is composed of many related individuals growing together as a community. The church as club or clan is a *congenial community* where personal relationships and traditions reign supreme. It can be visualized as a La-Z-Boy Recliner, where people relax after a tough time in the world. The church as charismatic-leader-and-followers is *a movement under command*, where the group ultimately depends on one person for its success and survival. It can be visualized as a Guided Missile, speeding toward a planned destination (but which sometimes hits the wrong target). The church as company or corporation is *an organization with a plan* which it works to achieve tangible goals. It can be visualized as a Factory that produces people with the proper knowledge, beliefs and behavior.

THE PROBLEM OF PLANNED CHANGE FOR THE CLUB OR CLAN

What do we do when a church doesn't seem to be "working" very well? That is, what do we do when declines in membership (or offerings) become serious enough to get our attention? A congregation may be getting older and cannot seem to attract any of the young families that are moving into the community. A long-tenured minister retires and the congregation doesn't think it can afford a full-time replacement. An automotive supply plant that employs a lot of church members shuts down and people move away in search of new jobs. Many of those who stay behind don't have enough money to pay their own bills, much less those of their church. A serious conflict occurs, leaving behind a weakened, demoralized congregation. Churches find themselves in crisis situations for many reasons. Perhaps the crisis should not have been such a surprise, but more often than not churches do not see the problem coming until it is already upon them.

The church as club or clan is the most prevalent type of congregation in the United States and Canada and is the least likely to recognize that it has problems (internal or external). As with most families, the typical strategy of the clan-like church is avoidance. The strong sense of belonging in the church as club or clan gives it a sense of permanence. It may be over a hundred-years-old and members think it will be there forever. Furthermore, the church as club or clan is only peripherally related to its local community context. It is a close knit group with a life of its own; it is not necessarily a community institution. If members leave the area and move to the suburbs, most drive back in. If newcomers to the surrounding community are not "like us," they will not be accepted—despite our rhetoric about being open to everyone. Changes in the community and slow declines in membership may not be noticed until there is a crisis or until a new pastor is called.

So what does the passive club or clan church in crisis do, once it can no longer remain in its prone position? The typical reaction is the "fix it" approach, and there is a great deal of advice available to help churches do just that. In fact, I would characterize most of the literature on church growth and congregational planning as variations of the "planning and fix it model of congregational change." If it's broke, you fix it. If it's directionless, you identify a few goals and point it in the right direction. This approach is doomed to failure for several reasons. First, planned change requires commitment and motivation. Planning, in and of itself, does not create the energy necessary to do the things necessary to fix specific problems. Second, from a systems perspective (see chap. 3), an observable breakdown in one area is more often than not caused by problems elsewhere in the system. So rushing in to fix a breakdown will require an inordinate amount of resources and tends to be followed by a breakdown elsewhere in the system.

Figure 2

TRADITIONAL STRATEGY FOR ACTIVATING A PASSIVE (CLUB OR CLAN) CHURCH

Put Structure and
Goals in Place
[Company or Corporation]

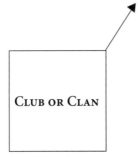

CLUB OR CLAN

Difficulties with a planning and fix it approach to congregational change are illustrated by figure 2. Advising a club or clan type church to refocus its vision, plan for its future, establish corporate goals, and redirect its energies is essentially asking it to move from the lower left cell to the upper right cell (to the church as company or corporation) in *one step*. It is trying to change a self-centered community with diffuse, intangible goals into a purposeful organization with very specific goals and objectives. Clubs and clans are about relationships; they are not about programs, plans, or goal setting.

It is too much to expect a group to change itself completely in two separate ways—for a church to establish a new selfless purpose and to replace its emphasis on community with a focus on specific, tangible goals. What happens when we try to make such changes? The same thing that happens in the corporate world among companies that are lost. Planning does not result in a plan, or it produces a plan that has no effect. A consultant comes in, diagnoses the problems, and outlines possible solutions. The church accepts the solutions and puts the structure and programs into place to do the job. The consultation event creates some excitement and for a while the church seems to have the energy to move forward on the consultant's recommendations. After a few months, however, almost always within a year, the excitement wears off and the congregation reverts to its old habits.[5] No change was made in the congregation's culture or even in its procedures. A *congenial community* cannot become an *organization with a plan* in a single step. The change is much too drastic and inertia is much too great. The only feasible possibility is for a church to change only *one* dimension at a time.

DIRECTIONS FOR THE CLUB OR CLAN

The church as club or clan can move to the right and become a charismatic-leader-and-followers or it can move directly upwards and become an incarnational community (see figs. 1 and 3). There is no reason for it to try to become a company or corporation. That strategy is doomed to fail and only replaces one set of problems with another.

---

5. C. Kirk Hadaway, "Do Church Growth Consultations Really Work?" *Church and Denominational Growth*, ed. David A. Roozen and C. Kirk Hadaway (Nashville, Tenn.: Abingdon Press, 1993), 149–54.

Figure 3

DIRECTIONS FOR CHANGE: THE CLUB OR CLAN

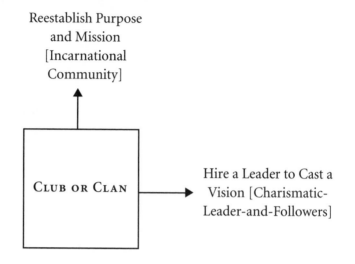

Reestablish Purpose
and Mission
[Incarnational
Community]

CLUB OR CLAN

Hire a Leader to Cast a
Vision [Charismatic-
Leader-and-Followers]

Most churches that fit the club or clan description are declining slowly in membership. A few others are plateaued. If any are growing, it is only because the group has a high birth rate and the children of church members are not moving away. All of the other three types contain substantial numbers of growing churches.

So if the church as club or clan wants to get out of its crisis, what should it do? The most direct approach is to move right to find a leader-savior who will attract new followers and stave off the crisis. This is not easy, of course, because the supply of potential charismatic leaders is quite limited—particularly in mainline denominations. White, mainline ministers, by and large, do not tend to be of the charismatic sort. Nevertheless, if a church manages to hire someone with the ability to attract followers, it soon faces another crisis. One of the key characteristics of the church as charismatic-leader-and-followers is that authority resides in the person of the pastor. But if a charismatic individual is hired only to save the church, authority may be withheld by long-term members. Two power structures tend to result from this situation: the pastor with her followers and the preexisting power structure that views the minister as their hired hand.

The new pastor may win the power struggle that develops; the new pastor may be terminated; or the power struggle may result in a split (or in disgruntled members leaving the church). In the first case, the church successfully moves from club or clan to charismatic-leader-and-followers. In the second case, the church reverts back immediately to the club or clan. In the third case, two churches may emerge: a club or clan and a charismatic-leader-and-followers.

Even though the church as club or clan might be seen as the worst of the four types in that it lacks purpose and isn't accomplishing anything, actually it is only one step away from becoming (or resuming life) as an incarnational community. In fact, this is the easiest direction for the church as club or clan to move, but recognizing how to change is not so obvious. Indeed, it is less about trying to change than about recognizing one's purpose and moving in whatever direction that purpose may lead.[6] More direct and obvious is to call an energetic pastor who will try to attract some new people.

Lack of specific goals is not the source of the difficulties faced by the church as club or clan. Nor is its problem the close-knit, family-like atmosphere that exists. A strong sense of community is an advantage, not a disadvantage. The problem lies in a lack of purpose. Its purpose has been displaced and must be put back in place.

It is so easy for a congregation to act like what it is not (a social club) that it sometimes forgets what it is (a church). The church as club or clan must be reminded of its true "business." It is not a social club but a religious organization, a community of faith that helps members have communion with God. It is a place where people have personal transformation, wake up to the reality of God's Realm, and begin to grow in knowledge and understanding in a vocational, incarnational life. It is not a place where people are left unchanged and self-satisfied.

Redirecting the church as club or clan is not about fixing anything. It is about realizing one's purpose (and undermining alternative, socially and denominationally affirmed, but essentially heretical, purposes). By necessity, this is a slow process which requires leaders to model and embody the

---

6. See Anthony de Mello, *Awareness: A de Mello Spirituality Conference in His Own Words*, ed. J. Francis Stroud (New York: Doubleday/Image Books, 1990), 145. Talking about people, rather than churches, de Mello says, "The harder you try to change yourself, the worse it gets. . . . Real change will come when it is brought about, not by your ego, but by reality. Awareness [seeing clearly] releases reality to change you." The bracketed words are mine.

undeluded life—to act like what they are, citizens of God's Realm who see things through fully opened eyes.

I am not talking about being artificial, perfectly controlled persons who cannot be emulated. That is the part played by a charismatic leader. The leader of an incarnational community, or the leader of a church that is moving in that direction, must only be open to the spirit of God and must expect God's Realm to break through—particularly in worship. Having all the answers and trying to live up to an ideal is not necessary. Being human is better. The only thing a leader must have that most members of a church as club or clan probably lack is an understanding of the church's purpose.[7] Why are we here? What does our present incarnation suggest about what we might become? The pastor and lay leaders of a church must answer those questions for themselves and help the rest of the congregation deal with them too.

When I presented this material to a group of Unitarian Universalist ministers, one responded, "but most people don't want to change!" It is true. A church sign I saw in Alabama says it well: "The only people who want to be changed are wet babies." Telling someone they need to change may provoke defensiveness and anger, like the reaction you may get when you tell your spouse or partner, "the problem with you is. . . ." The need to change is implied if we expect the church to be a place where people are transformed and grow in faith, but the emphasis should not be on our deficiencies—those things that cry out to be fixed. Emphasis should be on what we are becoming; it should be on what we are growing into. Church leaders are called to model that growth and the openness that it requires. There is no need to talk about the need to change. We can talk, however, about openness, transformation, and growth.

DIRECTIONS FOR THE CHARISMATIC-LEADER-AND-FOLLOWERS

The church as charismatic-leader-and-followers rarely recognizes the need to become something different, particularly when it is successful. The church is controlled by the leader, so unless the leader decides that change is necessary, the church will remain as it is.

---

7. In some cases, it is the lay leaders of a church that wants to change who call a pastor who shares their sense of purpose. They need a leader to provide direction, but the purpose is already there. A group of United Church of Christ laity and their newly called pastor reminded me of this truth during a workshop I conducted in Phoenix, Arizona.

A leader who recognizes the problem of dependency and leadership transition and who does not view the church as an extension of his being may work toward moving the church in the direction of a company or corporation. In Max Weber's terms, the leader may try to routinize his charisma by helping the church invest authority in the *position* of pastor rather than in the *person* of the leader. The charismatic leader also may try to institutionalize his vision for the church in the form of an ideology. If he is successful, the next pastor of the church may have less personal authority, but the church will have much more institutional strength. Specific goals will remain in place, but the goals are now connected to a belief system rather than to an individual.

The transition from charismatic-leader-and-followers to company or corporation is a necessary first step toward becoming an incarnational community because the church lacks the resources of a community-based culture. A clear purpose cannot be drawn from nor accepted by a culture that doesn't exist. Rather, purpose must be vested first in the structure of an organization. Members, playing roles they have been assigned, use the structure to achieve organizational goals. A wise leader then begins to help the institution develop a stronger community life and simultaneously undermines the tangible nature of the organization's goals—reminding members of the real goals of the church.

The church as charismatic-leader-and-followers cannot move directly to the incarnational community. It can move up (see figs. 1 and 4) and become a company or corporation or it can move to the left and become a club or clan. Moving left will not be intentional. The church will move in this direction if its efforts fail and it becomes more of a cult and less of a movement. If the leader dies without a successor, or if the leader somehow loses her charisma, the church may be left with a committed cadre of members who have given up everything to belong to the group. They will remain in it no matter what happens. Without a strong leader and her compelling vision, the group may continue to meet, although it remains a shadow of its former self. A once-charismatic leader may even continue to express her vision for the church, but members are not really listening anymore. The leader is only playing her part in a drama that has no real purpose and no specific objectives. The church continues to exist because of relationships and the fact that joining the group involved severing outside connections. It becomes a club or clan.

Figure 4

DIRECTIONS FOR CHANGE: THE CHARISMATIC-LEADER-AND-FOLLOWERS

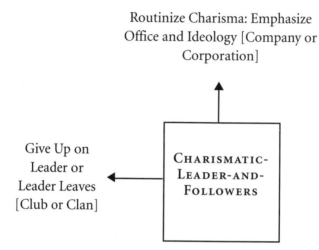

Routinize Charisma: Emphasize
Office and Ideology [Company or
Corporation]

Give Up on
Leader or
Leader Leaves
[Club or Clan]

CHARISMATIC-
LEADER-AND-
FOLLOWERS

DIRECTIONS FOR THE COMPANY OR CORPORATION

The church as company or corporation is only one step away from becoming an incarnational community, but it also is unlikely to recognize the need to move in that direction. Because it operates on a cause and effect production model, any problems it experiences will tend to be interpreted as things that need to be fixed. If the church is "graying," it clearly requires a better youth program or a new nursery. Putting the programs in place and providing adequate staffing will solve the problem and restore production. Membership declines are likely to be interpreted as failures in outreach or publicity—problems to be addressed by a direct mail campaign, a "bring a friend" Sunday, an organized visitation program, or public events that draw in people who don't normally attend church. There is nothing inherently wrong with doing any of these things, but if the flow of the system isn't working, new or revamped programs won't help.

When the church as company or corporation is growing and the budget is increasing—that is, when it has no obvious problems to address—the church is even less likely to see the need to change in any substantial way. If the church seems to be achieving its specific and tangible goals, why would it want to make its goals less specific? If it did so, what would happen to its sense of accomplishment and its feeling of being blessed by God with growth?

The church as company or corporation that is working smoothly is lifted up as an example of what a good church should be. It seems to be getting results. The problem is that a church should not have goals that are clear and easy to measure. It should not be obvious that a church is well organized and getting results, and if it is, we may then want to look closely at the nature of its product.

Attracting an audience into a setting for education and/or entertainment is not the same thing as growing disciples who have a faith that is their own. The church as company or corporation tends to mistake its structure and programs for the results they are designed to achieve. The church as company or corporation tends to misinterpret the meaning of the specific results that it gets. By looking at programs and structure as means to specific ends the church as company or corporation develops programs and structures that produce unintended results.

Religious education does not necessarily result in learning. A worship service does not necessarily result in communion with God. A sermon does not necessarily result in behavioral change. A social justice ministry does not necessarily result in dismantled injustice. An evangelism strategy does not necessarily result in lives changed by the gospel of Christ. However, it is possible to see the results of such programs and events as if they really did what was intended.

In order to move toward an incarnational community, the church as company or corporation must recognize that it is more than a production facility, more than a bureaucracy doing God's work, and more than a sacramental workstation. People can be transformed through the church in spite of inadequate programs and bad organizational structure. What matters most is the way we perform worship and approach ministry, not how they are structured. The worship, ministry, relationships, and life of the church should not be seen as a means to an end, but as ends in themselves. They should not be seen as efforts to control outcomes, because outcomes involving people can never be controlled. The incarnational community gives up control over outcomes and focuses on the doing of its ministry, on

Figure 5

DIRECTIONS FOR CHANGE: THE COMPANY OR CORPORATION

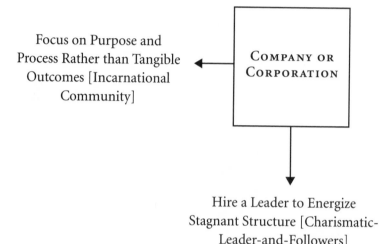

Focus on Purpose and Process Rather than Tangible Outcomes [Incarnational Community]

COMPANY OR CORPORATION

Hire a Leader to Energize Stagnant Structure [Charismatic-Leader-and-Followers]

fulfilling its vows. By giving up control and giving permission to members to begin new things, the diffuse outcomes—the transformations—which are natural for churches, tend to come naturally. They do not have to be forced.

It also is possible for the church as company or corporation to move down on the grid by becoming a charismatic-leader-and-followers. As illustrated in figure 5, this can happen when a bureaucratic church hires a charismatic leader to energize a stagnant structure. Under certain conditions a great preacher with a lot of ambition and clear sense of God's calling can slowly consolidate most of the power in the church. There may be no takeover, although this can happen as well. Usually, the process is not so abrupt. Eventually all of the decision-making structure operates only as a rubber stamp for the leader's wishes. Examples of this process can be observed in several large Southern Baptist churches that are now essentially controlled by charismatic leaders. These churches are two steps removed from the incarnational community and must face the inevitable crisis of leadership transition.

NO IDEAL TYPE

Churches are not "types." Types are abstract concepts. Churches are specific incarnations. However, three of the types may seem to be very real and the fourth may seem to be an unachievable ideal. It is not. So why do there seem to be so few incarnational communities out there? One reason is that the problems that remain in any church, no matter how good it is, always stand out more than the positive characteristics. The second reason is that we live in a deluded society where success is measured by control over outcomes. It should be no surprise, therefore, that few churches have a clear understanding of their purpose. Such an understanding is essential for becoming an incarnational community.

Becoming an incarnational community is not objectively difficult. Mostly it involves giving up control and remembering why churches exist. The dynamic model described here may help clarify what is keeping your church from moving in that direction. If you think the model seems too mechanistic, don't worry. Think about it like this: All churches have signs of life, flickering flames of hope. What is required is to fan those flames, to give sustenance to the life that is present now. The incarnational community will emerge when we allow it to do so, growing out of embers that are not yet cold.

Chapter six

LEADERSHIP FOR TRANSFORMATION

DON'T BE A MANAGER; be a leader! That is the advice given to ministers (and corporate CEOs). Other voices call for ministers to play a more religious role. They should be prophets. What is the proper role for a minister then? Maybe it should be that of a pastor—a role that would seem to combine direction (leadership), care (management), and rescuing the flock from harm (prophetic).[1]

The pastor is not the leader. A pastor *exercises leadership*. Leadership is a function, a process. It is not a thing, a person or a position. As Ronald Heifetz says, "leadership means influencing people to face their problems."[2] It is about leading an organization to put a "generative system" in place, a system with the transformational capacity to create the outcomes that aren't now happening.

Leadership is about direction and purpose. That is to say, a central task of the pastor (and of laity who also exercise leadership) is to keep the organization on mission, concentrated on the substance of its purpose—"to stick to its knitting," as business leaders like to say. An excellent pastor, above all, understands the purpose of the organization and consistently *embodies* that purpose in his actions and conversations.[3] By leading in an embodied way he guides members of the organization in the same direction, consistent with their purpose.[4]

---

1. Usually the problem is not a wolf. Rather, the prophetic role is to help the flock out of the ditch into which they have blundered. See Ronald A. Heifetz, *Leadership without Easy Answers* (Cambridge: Harvard University Press, 1994), 53, for an interesting discussion of the social origins of leadership.

2. Ibid., 14.

3. Embodying mission means to live out the organization's transformational purpose.

4. Not in the form of a movement. The mission of the church is primarily internal; resulting in transformed people and transformed action external to the group.

How is this directional guiding typically done? First, by remembering that he leads people, not sheep.[5] Churches are not passive in the sense that members are aimlessly milling around without strong relationships with other persons in the flock. People in social collectivities are never passive, and people in churches should never be treated as an audience of isolated individuals or family units who meet for worship. Churches are like tribes, with rich histories, embedded conflicts, unspoken rules, and expected patterns of behavior. They are cultural groups, but they can be led.

How does one lead a cultural group? Charisma is one way, but not the best way, and it is something that few ministers possess. Another way is to use the structure of the organization and the office of pastor, but this only works in bureaucratic congregations with long histories of strong pastoral control. A pastor cannot command most congregations by virtue of charisma or office.

Whatever authority the pastor seems to possess is a gift bestowed by members of the congregation. Even when members lack the power to hire and fire their pastor, they can undermine pastoral leadership by withholding their labor, attention, participation, and money. It is the same in the business world. According to Peter Drucker:

> Any CEO who believes he controls the organization is kidding himself. The people in the accounting department control you. The people in the plants control you. It's like Truman's statement when Eisenhower was elected President: "Poor Ike. He'll sit in that big office and push a button and nothing will happen!"[6]

In order to lead, a pastor or priest needs the cooperation and support of members. She must mobilize them to work together on problems they may not even realize that they have. They must become an organization that recognizes the source of their problems and with the capacity to solve them.

In the business world, the nearest analogous position to the pastor might be the general manager of a plant, who stands in a tenuous position between the larger corporation and her workers. The general manager must motivate plant workers but lacks the power to compel them to perform at

5. See Lee Bolman and Terrance Deal, *Reframing Organizations: Artistry, Choice, and Leadership* (San Francisco: Jossey-Bass, 1991), 130.

6. Peter Drucker, "Managing to Minister," *Leadership* (spring 1989): 22.

an optimal level. A manager must lead (rather than command) if she wishes to succeed. Studies of very successful general managers found certain common characteristics: *They were good at setting an agenda, building a network, and using that network to get things done.*[7] They did not plan, organize, motivate, or control in a formal way. Instead they acted informally by joking around and talking to people—frequently about non-work issues. Rarely did they seem to make decisions. Instead they led by trying to influence people. Sounds like a pastoral role to me!

PREPARING THE VESSEL

The first task of the pastor as general manager—setting the agenda—may sound too much like preparing for a committee meeting in a bureaucracy. But what is an agenda? It is a list of what we are going to deal with out of all the possible things we might consider. An agenda is about focus. Leadership is about helping the church focus on what is essential to its purpose.

In *Catalytic Leadership*, Jeffrey Luke says that the leader must "frame issues" in order to "crystallize thinking, focus attention, and stimulate discussion" so that the problem facing the organization stands out from all of the other tangential issues and concerns that it might address.[8] As much as it disturbs my Democratic sensibilities to say it, we can learn from Ronald Reagan's penchant for simplicity here. We should "shake off complications like a dog shakes off water." Oversimplification of complex issues should not concern us, as long as the agenda is not about an idealized vision of the future. The excellent leader "sets aside the weighty burden of an ultimate goal."[9]

The biggest obstacles facing older churches are established patterns of action (habits) which support goals that are either irrelevant to the purpose of the church or actually counter productive. Unless a leader is able to help the church reset its agenda, the purpose of changing lives will remain only one of many goals and may not receive much attention. As universities sometimes only make a reasonable stab at their primary goal of educating students, sometimes churches only make a reasonable stab at being religious institutions that transform lives. They cover the bases with warm bodies

---

7. Bolman and Deal, *Reframing Organizations*, 338.

8. Jeffrey Scott Luke, *Catalytic Leadership: Strategies for an Interconnected World* (San Francisco: Jossey-Bass, 1998), 63, 157.

9. Stanley M. Herman, *The Tao at Work: On Leading and Following* (San Francisco: Jossey-Bass, 1994).

and canned programs. All churches provide the basic elements of what a church is supposed to have: reasonably prepared worship, adequate Christian education for children, a full calendar of social events, hospital visitation by the pastor, and a structure for keeping the business running. By doing all this, they may delude themselves into thinking: "We are being the church." I would argue, however, that covering the bases only represents making a reasonable stab at their primary purpose and is clear evidence of goal displacement.

Some congregational scholars say that there are no bad churches—that all congregations have an integrity that is their own. This may be true, but I would counter by noting that many of these "good churches" have very bad habits—and by persisting in these habits they are unintentionally pursuing goals that have nothing to do with their stated purposes or theological understandings.[10] They are good institutions with faulty practices.

All organizations have many possible agendas to pursue. The pastor must help the congregation reduce, simplify, reframe, and refocus its agenda on key elements that are central to its purpose. Doing so takes clarity of vision (rather than a vision) and the willingness to give up peripheral things. Or perhaps "give up" is not the right way of expressing it. Attention and focus must not be deflected in these directions. The focus of church leadership must be on those tasks which are central to its purpose.

Obviously, church leaders must have clarity of vision before they can use it to help others see. Personal transformation is a prerequisite. It would not be helpful for the blind to lead the blind. But we cannot wait until we are fully aware of God's reality; we only become more aware of it through practice using our opening eyes. We begin exactly where we are through the spiral of transformation, allowing new insights to produce (in turn) new understanding, naturally-occurring changed behavior (words, actions, vocation), reinforcing practices, and transformed character (as citizens of God's Realm, open to new insights)—then back again. Like Jesus' disciples, we are dense, deluded people who are more comfortable within our well-worn ruts than we are in the uncharted territory outside them.[11] We must have the courage to put ourselves among the people/places/books where new

---

10. Peter Drucker, "Don't Change Corporate Culture—Use It!" *Wall Street Journal*, 28 March 1991, A14.

11. God's Realm is like the world outside the walls of a prison. The outside world is more real and natural than prisons built by human hands, but we are more familiar with the prison and understand its rules. The banquet outside is not well attended.

insights will begin the process of transformation, despite our best efforts to resist.

A key item on the agenda of a church becoming an incarnational community is preparing the transformational vessel for operation. We have inherited a breeder reactor that is no longer producing any energy or radioactive elements. It is just sitting there consuming dollars and providing work for its caretakers. What must we do to bring it back on-line, to release its unused energy? The specifics will vary from church to church, of course, but there are some key factors.

Ezra Earl Jones says there are only two primary tasks of the church, and each must be done well. The first is worship; the second is small groups.[12] Uplifting, transformational worship in which people experience communion with God, with God's people, in the reality of God's Realm, is a necessity for any church. Worship helps create a space for God to act in our lives—to break through the selves that we are trying to protect. It also provides the setting where the pastor can begin to apply the spark, the catalystic words, actions, and images that provoke new insights.

Small groups, or any form of community that enables members to know one another in non-superficial ways and form the church, are essential to the transformational vessel. In such settings, members are exposed to the personal influence and examples of other persons of faith. No one can grow into a disciple alone. The word "disciple" implies being influenced by another who serves as an example. In the church context we may have many examples, but in order for to them to influence us, in order for us to learn from them, we must know them and see the way in which their faith—their openness and trust—forms a part of their being. They need our example and we need theirs, not to imitate precisely, but to allow us to rub off on each other. Together we form a vessel that has the capacity to transform.

Patrick Keifert at Luther Seminary in St. Paul, Minnesota, has conducted research to confirm Jones's point. He found that members of growing churches (as opposed to declining and plateaued churches) spend proportionately more time in "dynamic public worship" and "significant relational

---

12. Taken from my notes on Ezra Earl Jones presentation to the working group on evangelism, National Council of Churches of Christ, held in Ashville, N.C., 1 Dec. 1994.

groups" and proportionately less time in "mediating structures" such as committees and business meetings.[13]

According to Jones and Keifert, our agenda should begin with changing our habits regarding how worship is conducted and the types of groups we nurture. This is how we prepare to put the dormant reactor back on line. Once the transformational process begins, heat and excitement will flow from the reaction, and a difference may be noticed in the lives of members and in the actions of the organization. Excess energy will be put to good use in the local community and beyond. The openness necessary for personal transformation may lead us in surprising directions—directions that transcend the usual outcome categories of evangelism and social justice. The boundaries of the Realm of God are not easily mapped.

STARTING A CHAIN REACTION

The church as company or corporation tries to control its outcomes. In the real world, however, outcomes cannot be controlled. Furthermore, trying to control our outcomes dampens the generative process that we want to create. It prevents the chain reaction from occurring. This generative principle is not limited to the diffuse outcomes of the church. A truly effective leader/manager/prophet in *any* organization is most interested in keeping the organization focused on its true business and in maintaining an environment where people do what they are best able to do in the best way they can.

Herb Kelleher, CEO of Southwest Airlines, describes his approach to management and control in this way:

> I've never had any control and I never wanted it. If you create an environment where people truly participate, you don't need control. They know what needs to be done and they do it. And the more that people will devote to your cause on a voluntary basis, a willing basis, the fewer hierarchies and control mechanisms you need. We're not looking for blind obedience. We're looking for people, who on their own initiative, want to be doing what they're doing because they consider it to be a worthy objective.[14]

---

13. From my notes on Pat Keifert's address to the United Church Board for Homeland Ministries.

14. Herb Kelleher, "A Culture of Commitment . . . Lessons from Southwest Airlines," *Leader to Leader* (spring 1997): 1.

Stanley Herman makes a similar point: "The excellent leader leads the least. He studies the distinctive skills and natural inclinations of [everyone] and he directs their attention to accomplish what is required to benefit all. When this has been done, all declare they have been part of a worthwhile purpose."[15] Whether you are the pastor of a church or a consultant conducting a congregational intervention process, the most effective outcome is when church members think they did everything themselves. Lack of proper credit to the pastor or consultant may bother those with weak egos, but not a leader who is more concerned about getting a taste of the cake everyone is baking together. Credit, honor, position, and just desserts are foreign concepts in God's Realm.[16]

Being the pastor of a church does not necessarily mean that you are the leader or can exercise much leadership. To use the analogy of the club or clan again: the pastor may play the role of clan priest. She may be called on to perform meaningful rituals and rites of passage at the appropriate times, but that does not mean she leads the clan. The primary leadership role—the chief—may be occupied already by someone who thinks they own the church, and perhaps in many ways they do. In churches lacking a chief, the tribe may be controlled by a group of powerful elders who require a religious functionary to do their bidding. In either case, the pastor is not expected to lead and her efforts to do so may be blocked.

Entering into a new pastorate and after a few months of living in a congregation, a new pastor may see problems standing out in high relief: "Why on earth do they do things like that here?" or "Why doesn't anyone other than me see the problem?" The answer is that it's kind of like the yellow crud on your stove or the black mold on your bathroom wall. It builds up so slowly over time that it's not noticeable until it really looks disgusting—but a visitor might see it immediately.

Before rushing in and trying to make major changes—to scrape up all the crud and throw it away—we should realize that "most people, most of

---

15. Herman, *The Tao at Work*, 38. Herman alternates male and female pronouns in his book as I do here. This just happens to be one occasion where the leader is called "he."

16. We need to get over it! as Leonard Sweet likes to say. Anthony de Mello likens the need for credit, approval, appreciation, attention, just rewards, and so on to addictive drugs. We are all addicted to them and the role of the church is to get the monkey off our backs—so we can live transformed lives. See de Mello, *Awareness: A de Mello Spirituality Conference in His Own Words*, ed. J. Francis Stroud (New York: Doubleday/Image Books, 1990), 162–64.

the time, are unaware of the discrepancy between what they intend and what they do."[17] They don't notice the problems, and in a few years a pastor may be trained so well that she won't notice them either. The problems will be part of the woodwork, part and parcel of the church and its identity. In other words, it is likely that the church will not realize its goal displacement. The church also may not be intrinsically opposed to a proper purpose. Members have simply gotten out of the habit of pursuing an agenda based on their purpose.

The pastor cannot command such an organization to change. The pastor must lead members to an awareness of what the function of the church should be, and she must do so within a structure of entrenched power and influence that may hinder (or help) her efforts. The church, like all other social groups, is not a machine that has been constructed to perform specific tasks. It is a living thing that has grown. It cannot be taken apart, fixed, and reassembled like an automobile engine, but it can be fertilized, pruned, and its growth can be guided. Future growth will only emerge from what is already there.

In order to exercise leadership, a pastor needs friends and allies who share similar perceptions of what the purpose of the church is. It also helps if some of those people have power and influence in the congregation. Lacking the support of a network, the pastor may remain in the position of clan priest or hired hand. Or, if he tries to force a new agenda on an unwilling power structure, he might be out of a job or marginalized within the congregation.

In a long-stagnant Baptist church in Springdale, Arkansas, the new pastor began visiting people in the small city who were known to be unchurched. Beginning alone, after a few weeks he asked a sympathetic church member to accompany him. Despite their rhetoric, few Baptist churches have the energy and commitment to do much evangelism. This pastor had both the energy and commitment, and he believed that evangelism should be central to the mission of any church. Through the efforts of this pastor and a few interested laypersons, many unchurched people in the community came to see God in a new way and were baptized into church membership. Baptisms were held on Sunday mornings, rather than Sunday night, so that more people (in the church and the community) could see how lives were

---

17. Bolman and Deal, *Reframing Organizations*, 240.

being changed. Friends and family members came and saw the transformation for themselves.

Slowly, more and more people in the congregation became excited about what was happening. People were coming to know Christ, church members were learning how to share their faith, and more and more new people—some well-known for their previous ill feelings about the church—were joining. Through this process, the pastor developed a large support base.

Some powerful, long-term members of the church were not excited about the changes, however. The traditional, reverent worship services had become a bit too enthusiastic. Some of the new members didn't dress very well and spoke up in business meetings when they should have kept quiet. They had never been trained in proper church etiquette. It also became clear that a new sanctuary would be necessary if growth continued. The church was not the same.

According to Lee Bolman and Terrance Deal, change in an organization "alters power relationships and undermines existing agreements and pacts. Most important, it intrudes upon deeply rooted symbolic agreements and ritual behavior."[18] The existing power structure of the congregation did not like what was happening to their church and began to criticize the pastor. He was very hurt by the grumbling and confused by the reaction to what he thought were good things and basic to the purpose of an evangelical church. He considered leaving.

The criticism never led to a leadership crisis, however, because too many people identified with the transformation—including many long-term members. Also, it was difficult for disgruntled members to attack openly a Baptist pastor who was reaching unchurched persons for Christ. Eventually, most of the worst critics were won over. They realized the church had become something better, even though they had to give up their cozy club/clan congregation. A few persons did leave, but not many.

We may think we know the formula for reforming any messed up church. We are wrong. We can't have ultimate knowledge of the organization we are trying to change, and we can't predict the outcome of our intervention. What we can do is help prepare the vessel for change by changing the way we do things, and we can act as the catalyst for change in others. In his book *Sustaining Innovation*, Paul C. Light suggests that all organizations contain

---

18. Ibid., 376.

the seeds to become "awesome vessels of power." Helping them realize the potential contained in those seeds is the leader's job. The way to do it is "definitely not to do the planning, ordering, or controlling, but to provide the spark (or sun and rain if you will) that would allow these awesome vessels of power already inside the organization to [grow]."[19]

Even when the proper structure is in place, and even when people say they understand the transformational purpose of the church, someone must supply the *spark* to get the chain reaction going. It is the reaction within the containment vessel that begins to transform people, not what the minister tells them they should do or even good-intentioned efforts by members to change themselves. By living a life that is being transformed, providing insights and provocations in worship, and sharing his life with people, the pastor helps spark the reaction. In some cases, the reaction may already be there, sputtering along among laity who can't reach critical mass by themselves. The pastor brings these like-minded souls together and something begins to happen. Eventually, more and more people start to "get it." They suddenly understand why their church exists. They had forgotten! Once they understand the purpose of the church, structural change becomes easier. The worship service can be adjusted; furniture can be moved; artwork put up or taken down. Resistance is reduced because people begin to trust one another—and God. Members and visitors sense that they are in the midst of something (that they are creating) which allows them and everyone else to experience God's reality. It is a transforming taste, an enlightening glimpse of a feast.[20] They want some more of it and they are willing to do what it takes to get their full measure.[21]

GENERATING HEAT

When people are being transformed they see things differently—in their own lives and in the world around them. They may ask themselves, "Why am I living like this?" and they may ask their pastor, "Why can't something be done about that"? We are producing unstable charged particles with the

---

19. Paul C. Light, *Sustaining Innovation: Creating Nonprofit and Government Organizations that Innovate Naturally* (San Francisco: Jossey-Bass, 1998), 137.

20. See Matthew 22:1–14.

21. The image here is of Germans in a beer hall, pounding their steins on wooden tables, shouting "full measure" at bartenders filling steins with more beer.

energy to transform others around them. What should we do? We should not leave them alone in their confusion and allow their energy to dissipate. We want to keep the reaction going (changing them and changing others) and allow the excess heat to be put to good use. Keeping the reaction going and using the excess heat involves (among other things) education and ministry action.

The church provides the containment vessel for a process of continuous transformation. The community network formed within has the capacity to transform people. The process never stops. Transformation is never finished, though it is always complete.[22] It begins with new insights, "a-has," jarring statements that shake us up—like a doctor telling us we have a tumor that just might kill us. With a newly-acquired perspective on life, we want to understand what has happened to us and what we should do. The educational ministries of the church (formal and informal) provide the interpretation of our experience, and the practices of the church suggest a path for integrating it into our lives. Waking up and seeing our delusions for what they are may not seem as shocking as hearing that we have cancer, but what could be worse than realizing that the things we had been striving for all of our lives were *keeping us* from the satisfaction we thought they would provide? What could be worse than realizing that the doors to our prison cells had been open all the time? The initial jolt of transformation is the most difficult part of the process—there is a lot of resistance and inertia to overcome. Keeping transformation going, once it begins, is much easier. It is mostly a matter of helping people create lives of openness rather than of control. They learn how to remain open to new insights that fire and fan the transformational process.

As noted earlier, church leaders and denominational officials always seem more interested in the inviting and the sending than in the transformation that energizes both. Transformation can occur through evangelism and social ministry, but most people will not be motivated to participate in either until something has happened to change them into people who want to do such things. There are few natural zealots in your congregation and guilt trips and pleading will not change the situation. Figure 6 suggests how ministries emerge naturally from transformational processes.

---

22. The specific incarnation that results from transformation is perfect, complete, and able to function accordingly. It is always in the process of becoming something new, however.

Figure 6

TRANSFORMATION AND MINISTRY ACTION

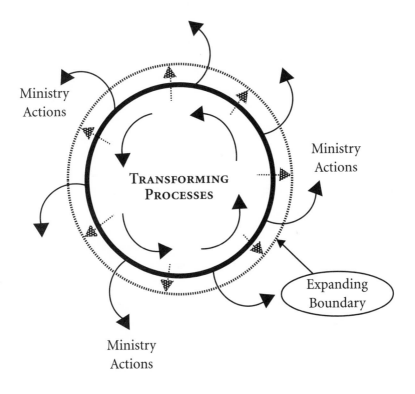

Ministry
Actions

Ministry
Actions

**TRANSFORMING
PROCESSES**

Expanding
Boundary

Ministry
Actions

The task of church leadership is to spark the transformational process and then allow members to work out of their own transformations, individually and collectively through emerging ministries of the church.[23] These ministries cannot be predicted and there should be no hard and fast rules about what is appropriate for the church. A lot depends on the specific incarnation of the church at that moment and what it is "tuned" or "tooled" to do. Bill Easum describes how the process might operate in an "organic church," organized around purpose. Such a church would have a team that

23. Bernard Glassman and Rick Fields, *Instructions to the Cook: A Zen Master's Lessons in Living a Life that Matters* (New York: Bell Tower, 1996), 128.

"must give permission to anyone who felt called to do anything that enhanced the mission. . . . Before telling someone 'no,' the [team] would have
to justify the decision."[24]

Church leaders cannot really control anything anyway, so they should
encourage lack of control. A certain amount of chaos is good—and by this
I mean that the church should be more permission-giving than nay-saying.
New ministry directions cannot be anticipated so they shouldn't be
planned.[25]

In his book, *The Purpose Driven Church*, Rick Warren writes about how
ministries develop in his congregation. He says, "the staff at Saddleback
never starts new ministries. We may suggest an idea, but we let the idea
percolate until God provides the right person to lead it."[26] He goes on to say
that his church did not have organized youth or singles ministries until
several hundred persons were already involved in these areas.

As an example of empowerment, Rick told this story:

> Someone once told me, "I've been feeling so burdened for the people in prison
> that I've been going out there to lead a Bible study. I think the church should
> do something for those people." I said to him, "It sounds to me like the church
> did do something. You are the church!" The next week I told the whole con-
> gregation, "I release all of you to visit those in prison, feed the hungry, clothe
> the poor, and shelter the homeless—and you don't even have to tell me. Just
> do it! Represent the church in Jesus' name." Help people realize that they are
> the church.[27]

One might fault Saddleback Community Church or its organized ministry priorities, but that is not the point. The point is the way the church
allows ministries to emerge. The youth, singles, and prison ministries of the
church were not planned, they just erupted because members were empowered to do something that they were concerned about and that fit the
overall mission of the church. Organization, in the form of staff involvement and budget came later, after the idea was already incarnated in the

---

24. William A. Easum, "If I Were a Pastor Again," *Net Results* (July 1997): 16.

25. Obviously, this is an overstatement made to emphasize a point.

26. Rick Warren, *The Purpose-Driven Church: Growth without Compromising Your Message
and Mission* (Grand Rapids, Mich.: Zondervan, 1995), 384.

27. Ibid., 386.

form of ministry activities that energized certain members of the church. Too often we begin the opposite way, with organization (structure) and then expect members to volunteer for the needed leadership roles. Is it any wonder that so many ministries never take off?

Another illustration of how unexpected ministries emerge is provided by the Church of the Open Door, a predominantly black gay/lesbian congregation, located in a predominantly Hispanic neighborhood a few miles from Midway Airport in Chicago.[28] It is a "special purpose" church, drawing members from all over the city and even from neighboring states. Few people from the local community attend worship at the church, but that does not mean the church is uninvolved in their lives. The church saw itself as part of the local community from the beginning. Local people were hired as support staff. The church worked with its neighbors and police to end drug dealing on neighborhood streets (mostly by outsiders to outsiders). As their relationship developed with the community, other needs became apparent. The church now has a large day care program, literacy classes, citizenship classes, and a computer lab for occupational training. The church is alive with activity every day of the week. What kind of a church is this? It is both a neighborhood church and a special purpose, regional congregation—a hybrid that could not be planned. And what does the future hold? Community residents now want the church to start Spanish-language Bible studies for them and the co-pastors are talking about adding a Hispanic minister to the staff.

A permission-giving approach extends beyond decisions about which ministries to pursue. It also should carry over into the operation of the ministries themselves. Volunteer leaders should be able to lead the tasks they accept from the church. They must be allowed to make their own decisions with only general oversight from the church council or staff. They should not have to get approval to make needed changes or to use the resources that are budgeted for the ministry. People develop ownership, and with ownership comes a personal investment in how the ministry evolves. It is not a chore or an assignment. It is their ministry. You do not need to be excited about it. It is enough that *they* are excited about it. All the pastor has to do is provide encouragement, a system that allows the freedom to try new things, and the wisdom not to interfere.

---

28. They prefer "black" to "African American."

Most organizations fear this kind of lack of control. Leaders have heard too many horror stories about small groups veering into heresy or powerful cliques emerging to threaten the power of the pastor. These things can happen, but the threat they pose is much less probable than that the church will begin to make a reasonable stab at ministries that seem most appropriate. I also would add that the problems that can arise when ministry groups go out of control result more from lack of proper attention than lack of control and when the operative purpose of the group begins to shift. Ministry groups can suffer goal displacement in the same way as the larger congregation, and it is the role of the pastor and the church community to make sure group leaders continue to understand why their group exists.

To quote Rick Warren again:

> Expect the best of your people and trust them with ministry. Many people are so afraid of *wildfire* that they spend all their time putting out every little campfire that'll warm up the church! If you're the pastor, let others make some of the mistakes! Don't insist in making them all yourself. You bring out the best in people by giving them a *challenge*, giving them *control*, and giving them the *credit*.[29]

Will all these new ministries succeed? No. But we should not be afraid of failure or treat it as the end of the world when it happens. Perhaps we should institutionalize the expectation that some ministry ideas will fail. A good example is given by Warren Keating at First Presbyterian Church, Derby, Kansas, who "encouraged each group, committee, church school class, women's circle, session [even himself] to achieve two failures. The idea freed up people to try new and innovative ministries, programs, fellowship activities, classes, etc.—without any stigma attached if the project failed." He provided further encouragement through the church's newsletter, his sermons, and in personal conversations. The message communicated was "we need to try new things: to walk on the edge of creativity so that we sometimes fail." He says it worked. "Folks are excited about trying new things. How can they lose? If an idea doesn't work out, they smile and say: "This is one of our failures!"[30]

---

29. Warren, *The Purpose-Driven Church*, 388.
30. Warren J. Keating, "Success Requires Failure," *Net Results* (May 1998): 13.

Visualize the church as a living thing, as a fruit tree if you will, to be nurtured, guided, and gently pruned. It is not a machine to be fixed. Without proper attention and purposeful action it may become overgrown and unproductive, or it may shrivel and die. A general idea about how you want it to grow—its general shape—is the correct approach, but don't expect it to develop exactly as you imagine. *Let it find its own unique form.*

The church needs leadership to help bring habits in line with purpose, so it can "stick to its knitting." Without empowering, permission-giving leaders who embody the congregation's mission, it is likely that the church will make only a reasonable stab at the basic tasks all churches are supposed to do.

Because the pastor cannot command, he or she must *lead*. Proper leadership involves helping church members remember the purpose of the church, helping spark a chain reaction in receptive areas of the congregation and helping nurture the transformational process and channel the heat it produces. The pastor cannot order members to do what must be done, nor can she effect change directly. Instead, the minister must lead the congregation to solve their own problems by creating a breeder reactor in which constituent elements transform each other. The transformed elements then enable other elements to be transformed. It is a generative process, to which all contribute, and through which all gain. The reaction also generates a lot of heat that the church does not waste. It is put to good use outside the walls of the transformational vessel.

Chapter seven

WORDS FOR LIBERATION

A talent for speaking differently, rather than for arguing well, is the chief instrument of change.

—Richard Rorty[1]

WORSHIP IS A PROCESS where all of our actions combine for a singular, communal purpose. It would make sense, then, for the sermon be a part of that assembling process, rather than standing apart as a presentation to be received, enjoyed or endured. As Aidan Kavanagh says, "The homily must not separate word and sacrament but unite them."[2]

A worship service is not like a concert with an opening act and a main event. Worship is more like a raft ride down a mountain river, with exciting passages that leave us breathless and calm places where we sit and contemplate—with bends and curves where we cannot see where we are going. Yet it also is a river that we have gone down before. Each time we repeat the experience, memories of past trips are evoked. We anticipate what will come next, but every ride is different, depending on the season, the strength of the current, and our traveling companions. We may not experience fear in church, and screaming is usually discouraged, but we should experience something, perhaps even something out of the ordinary, before we finish the trip and pull out of the river.

My last raft ride was down the Snake River in Wyoming, outside Grand Teton National Park. I remember many things about it. I can still feel the rush of the water. I remember the bald eagle in her nest, the snag that almost caught our raft, the dramatic views of the Teton Range rising up from

---

1. Richard Rorty, *Contingency, Irony, and Solidarity* (New York: Cambridge University Press, 1989), 7.

2. Aidan Kavanagh, *Elements of Rite: A Handbook of Liturgical Style* (Collegeville, Minn.: Liturgical Press, 1990), 51.

the plain, and my companions trying to take pictures without falling into the river. I know what I saw and what I felt, but I don't remember much about what our guide said as he described the geology of the valley and the animals that live in the park.

Because the typical worship service does not have the grandeur of the Grand Teton range, a great responsibility is placed upon the minister and her sermon. If people are to be affected, changed, or transformed, it is left up to her to do it—to bring a message that will touch their hearts. It is like elevating a river guide's nature lecture over the full-bodied experience of the ride down the river.

Interpretive words are helpful, but they are most effective when they do not have to stand alone and point to an experience that people are not having. They are most effective when they engage the mind in such a way as to make the overall experience—the raft ride—even more meaningful. Words prepare us to use more than our minds and, when used well, they help us become more than passengers who are along for the ride. We become interpreters of our own experience when words "infect one with a cerebral itch which compels one to scratch up insights of various kinds."[3]

EDUCATION, MOTIVATION, OR ALLEVIATION

The typical sermon is an effort to *educate, motivate,* or *alleviate.* Some sermons try to do all three. Very few sermons help *liberate,* a process which, it seems to me, is the primary reason we require churches and religion. We need to be saved, not from hell in the life hereafter, but from a deluded life apart from God's present (eternal) reality. It is to this new life we are called and to which we call others.

In the words of Paul Tillich:

Salvation happens whenever the enslaving power is conquered, whenever the wall is broken through, whenever the sickness is healed. He who can do this is called the saviour. . . . Whenever [salvation] appears, it is a manifestation of eternal, divine life in our temporal and mortal existence. All liberators are sent by God. . . . Who are these healers? Who are these liberators?

---

3. Kavanagh, *On Liturgical Theology* (New York: Pueblo Publishing, 1984), 73.

The first answer is: They are here; they are you. Each one of you has liberating power over someone to whom you are a priest. We are all called to be priests to one another; and if priests, also physicians. And if physicians, also counselors. And if counselors, also liberators.[4]

Amen! We want to liberate people from bondage so that they can experience new life. In our desire to help people, we tend to forget that liberation or transformation is a process that cannot be pursued directly. It is a cycle that we must engage and cultivate. It is not something that can be forced by telling people about an ideal state of being for which they need to strive. Yet this is what we do.

HELP THAT DOESN'T HELP

Most sermons address basic human problems and offer information and answers. We have a tendency to_____. Fill in the blank. We give up hope, we sin, forget the costs of discipleship, hold grudges, don't forgive (ourselves and others), can't see the mystery of God, over-consume, ignore injustice in the world, and so on.

When I sit in churches and listen to sermons, I usually agree with the minister—"Yeah, that's what I do," and if there is a scripture reading, I see that people have been doing this thing for thousands of years. When the sermon shows me the implications of my actions, I also see how doing them (or not doing them) messes up my life and helps reinforce social conditions that hurt everyone.

The hard part—always—is to come up with something to do about our predicament. We want to provide some answers or some marching orders. We want to wrap it up in a nice package like the kindly parent in a 1950s television show. But the answers don't "take," or at least not for very long. I listen and think I am not Mother Teresa, Billy Graham, or Malcolm X. I'm just a guy with a moderately dysfunctional life, trying to grab a little fun and fulfillment along the way. So I listen to the answers and orders and think, "I *can't* do that," "Well, that sounds laudable, but I don't *want* to do that," or "*What* are you talking about?" I shake my head, leave, and continue doing or not doing the things that were the subject of the sermon.

---

4. Paul Tillich, *The Eternal Now* (New York: Scribner, 1963), 115.

On a recent Sunday I went to worship services at two different churches and listened to the sermons. One dealt with our tendency to give up hope. The other dealt with keeping God inside a box of conventional assumptions. One minister was very conservative; the other was mainline. I recognized the problems that both ministers addressed. Sometimes I give up hope. I give up on people. I give up on God. I also want God to fit the image that I adopted as a child—a God who is supposed to take care of me and my life before worrying about other people. I saw the implications of giving up hope and holding onto my pet God. But what were the answers and the orders? In the first sermon I was told not to give up hope because "help was on its way!" The solution was illustrated by the story of a man who was digging in the hills for gold, gave up, and then woke up the next day to find that a rainstorm had uncovered a gold mine in his yard. I don't mean to be overly critical, but to me the point of the story was that perhaps we should give up. But even if the story had been about someone who did not give up, it still wouldn't have helped me. I did not learn how to keep hoping. I was just told to do it.

The second sermon also gave me some answers and told me what to do. The story here used Jonah as a negative example. We are not to do what Jonah did. We have a choice, the minister said, to cling to our current, conventional assumptions about God, or to explore new territory with new assumptions. I agreed wholeheartedly, but how do I do it? For someone who thinks inside the box it is very difficult to think outside, and being told that it's a good thing doesn't help. Somewhat more helpful was the minister's point that if we look closely at our lives, we can see that God rarely acts in ways that we expect. So even though I wasn't told specifically to look for the ways God is working unexpectedly in my life, I took that as something I could do.

These were not bad sermons. I enjoyed hearing both of them. I listened (obviously), paid attention, and got the points. That doesn't always happen. Like many people today, I have a rather short attention span and a tendency to daydream. So I frequently fade in and out of sermons and lectures, getting only a disjointed sense of what the message was about. I got both messages that Sunday, but they didn't get me. I was unchanged, unaffected and, if anything, more frustrated than before because I have a heightened awareness of two problems in my life without a meaningful solution.

BETTER ANSWERS OR A DIFFERENT PROCESS?

We have a tendency to pose direct, fix it solutions to embedded, systemic problems. It's like a parent helping their child with the problem of thumb sucking. We tell them that it's a disgusting habit; we explain why they shouldn't do it and then we say, "don't do that anymore." Simply telling someone what he or she shouldn't be doing or what they ought to be doing does not result in lasting change.

So why do we persist in the telling? It is because we see things in terms of cause-and-effect, rather than as emerging from the interaction of patterns and events. We introduce a cause in the form of a directive or a suggestion, hoping for the desired effect. Why do we think this way? We might blame it in part on Gutenberg and the transformation of knowledge—from something gained through the experience of it to a set of instructions transmitted through the written word.[5] Words marching across the page reinforce a linear view of life, in which one event leads to another, rather than the reality of events unfolding in surprising ways. Real life is spontaneous and messy. We want to get it under control and try to do so by our actions and our admonitions to others.

If we really think about it, however, we realize that personal change does not happen all at once, even when a person decides to do something differently. Decisions are our way of naming the direction we are already going or of recognizing that we are becoming people who see life differently and are acting accordingly. As Anthony de Mello says, "change takes place through you, in you. *You* don't do it."[6] Real change cannot be instructed and we are fooling ourselves if we believe that something we said had a direct, causal effect on someone's life. We cannot change or liberate anyone. Even Jesus could not do that. But like Jesus we can serve as catalysts for change by proclaiming liberation (the Kingdom of God is at hand) and by giving people new images that react violently with the notions, beliefs, and habits that keep them in bondage.

---

5. Aristotle, Thomas Aquinas, and their inheritors also may be implicated.

6. Anthony de Mello, *Awareness: A de Mello Spirituality Conference in His Own Words*, ed. J. Francis Stroud (New York: Doubleday/Image Books, 1990), 84.

TO SEE AND EXPERIENCE

We should not help people who are in bondage feel better about their captivity. We do not need seminars on how to live more productively inside our prisons. We also do not need to rail against our bondage. We built our prisons ourselves.[7] But they are not real. We can see them for what they are and then get about the business of living as new (transformed) creatures within God's Realm (the real world).

In the story below, de Mello substitutes the image of being in prison with that of drowning in the sea:

> What exactly does Jesus mean by the Kingdom of God?
> Seeing Reality as it is.
> Doesn't everyone see Reality as it is?
> Oh no! Most people see it as they think it is.
> What's the difference?
> The difference between thinking you are drowning in a stormy sea—and knowing you cannot drown because there isn't any water for miles around.[8]

We require liberation into a new state of seeing and being. That is the core purpose of the church—to be a collection of people who are about the business of letting God's reality burst through the walls of their prisons. Our cells cannot contain both God and us, so something must give way.

The problem that we face in the third millennium is the same that Jesus faced in the first century. We live in a world in which social institutions and social conventions (including religion) keep us from knowing God and God's reality—and consequently from experiencing life in its fullness. Our efforts to cobble together a satisfying life sets up a vicious cycle of action-and-reaction directed at reaching a destination that never arrives. Even when we achieve some measure of success, it never seems like enough. When we

---

7. Real prisons of various kinds exist, of course, and I don't mean to minimize the presence of physical pain, emotional suffering, or social injustice. Clarity about the meaning of our own pain or the pain of others (and what to do about it) does not arise spontaneously, however. We must be able to see clearly in order to act appropriately and the social order that gave rise to the conditions that cause pain are unlikely to provide much enlightenment about appropriate actions and reactions.

8. Adapted from de Mello, *More One Minute Nonsense* (Chicago: Loyola University Press, 1993), 167.

get our lives under control, some new problem always crops up to throw us off balance. The only logical answer seems to be to work harder, act better, and to encourage others to do likewise. Jesus poses a more radical answer, however. He compels us to see the destructive cycle for what it is—and invites us to disengage ourselves from it.

The problem is that people cannot be argued out of an old way of seeing and being. Adults like you and me are fully-formed, hardened systems, complete with behavioral and perceptual patterns that more or less work and that we accept as right. When we are given new information—even radical new information—we try to incorporate it into our old ways of seeing and being. "One will seek to translate it immediately into the comfortable normalcy of one's ordinary . . . world."[9] Like the disciples at the Transfiguration, we want to house mystery in old confining categories.

The only way to engage the cycle of transformation into a new way of seeing and being is by disrupting our hardened, taken-for-granted understandings of reality. That is exactly what Jesus did. The purpose of Jesus' proverbs and parables were disruption, not instruction. They "challenge the hearer, not to radical obedience, but to radical questioning."[10] They were verbal "hand grenades" thrown by Jesus to blow up our settled, taken-for-granted worlds—our comfortable prisons.

Blowing up old worlds is not enough, however. Telling people they are free is not enough, either. We can rebuild our prisons and crawl back inside in an instant. So what can we do to engage the cycle of transformation once old patterns are disrupted? Again, the parables and proverbs of Jesus provide a model.[11] According to Norman Perrin, "the parables of Jesus were much more than illustrations explaining a difficult point, or telling weapons in a controversy; they were *bearers of the reality* with which they were concerned." They provoke a disconnection with the old and they evoke—in "prediscursive form"—a vision of the new.[12] It is not enough to tell some-

---

9. John Dominic Crossan, *In Parables: The Challenge of the Historical Jesus* (Sonoma, Calif.: Eagle Books, 1973), 12.

10. Norman Perrin, *Jesus and the Language of the Kingdom: Symbol and Metaphor in New Testament Interpretation* (Philadelphia: Fortress Press, 1976), 52.

11. It is possible, of course, to domesticate the parables and remove their radical character. Rather than trying to make sense out of them, we should ask why they don't make sense, at least within the bounds of social convention.

12. "Image" and "vision" are inadequate ways of conceptualizing an experience. It is a flash of insight that we try to "see" or imagine and then try to put into words.

one about the new reality, we have to be jolted (transfigured) into it so we can experience the reality for ourselves.

God's reality can only be experienced. It cannot be described. When we are present in it, we see our old worlds clearly and how they held us captive. We see the structure and walls that kept us inside. But because God's Realm is not constructed of concepts and has no ideal form, we cannot use concepts to capture its image. We see it; we taste it; we experience it fully from within. And when we know God's reality, we want others to know it too. So we stand with Jesus in that reality, try to expose the unreality for what it is, and show others the Kingdom.

Fortunately, the ability to experience God's reality is made easier, according to Elizabeth Dryer, by the fact that "God is already present in the world in more ways and more intimately than we can imagine. The primary task . . . is to 'uncover,' 'evoke,' or 're-represent' the presence of God."[13] The sermon or homily helps do just that.

IMAGES, OLD AND NEW

Earlier this year I posed this question to Robert Marrone, pastor of St. Peter Church in Cleveland: "Do you have any conscious sense of what you are trying to do when you compose your homilies?" He responded, "Trying to reshape the way they imagine, I would think." He went on to explain:

> A favorite teacher of mine used to say, "no one can believe in something that they can't imagine." And by "imagine" she means the power to change. The only real way change happens in people is when their images change—in the way they imagine things to be. So it seems to me that the homily does the same thing that the liturgy is supposed to do. It invites us to imagine a different world.
>
> [A homily] is all about chipping away at our given images and offering alternative images. The most memorable homilies are those when someone has offered you an image that names your experience and yet offers you a possibility of something else.[14]

---

13. Elizabeth A. Dreyer, *Earth Crammed with Heaven: A Spirituality of Everyday Life* (New York: Paulist Press, 1994), 110.

14. Personal interview with Robert Marrone at St. Peter Church, Cleveland, Ohio, 27 Jan. 1999.

We want to tell people the truth, so the truth can set them free. We have a problem, however, because as De Mello tells us, "truth is never expressed in words. Truth is sighted suddenly."[15] Truth shakes us to the very core of our being when the ring of recognition creates a harmonic resonance within us. In worship, we use more than words to sing that internal hymn, but words also can be used as a skillful means whereby truth is evoked. Our words can be more than words; they can weave stories and myths that do not so much as "capture" truth for us, as to release it in our imaginations.[16]

Christian worship centers on Biblical texts, and the object of the liturgy of the word is to open these readings and the images they contain with the congregation—together, as the people of God. The problem we face in using familiar readings is that we have ridden them too often. We have tamed the wildness out of them. Simply reading them and presenting a new interpretative twist won't do it. Sometimes we must retell the stories in order to restore their transforming character—so that they can give us new images that release the truth that was intended.

In the following passage, Marc Gellman evokes a new (and very old) sense of how people relate to God and God's world by retelling the story of creation:

> Before there was anything, there was God, a few angels, and a huge swirling glob of rocks and water with no place to go. The angels asked God, "Why don't you clean up this mess?"
>
> So God collected rocks from the huge swirling glob and put them together in clumps and said, "Some of these clumps of rocks will be planets, and some will be stars, and some of these rocks will be . . . just rocks."
>
> Then God collected water from the huge swirling glob and put it together in pools of water and said, "Some of these pools of water will be oceans, and some will become clouds, and some of this water will be . . . just water."
>
> Then the angels said, "Well God, it's neater now, but is it finished?" And God answered . . . "NOPE!"

---

15. de Mello, *Awareness*, 84.

16. Elizabeth Dreyer, *Earth Crammed with Heaven*, 68, says, "'myth' is the polar opposite of what is false. A 'myth' is a story about realities whose truth is so profound that only a story can begin to capture it. Ordinary, everyday language is simply not adequate to capture it."

On some of the rocks God placed growing things, and creeping things, and things that only God knows what they are, and when God had done all this, the angels asked God, "Is the world finished now?" And God answered: "NOPE!"

God made a man and a woman from some of the water and dust and said to them, "I am tired now. Please finish up the world for me . . . really it's almost done." But the man and woman said, "We can't finish the world alone! You have the plans and we are too little."

"You are big enough," God answered them. "But I agree to this. If you keep trying to finish the world, I will be your partner."

The man and the woman asked, "What's a partner?" and God answered, "A partner is someone you work with on a big thing neither of you can do alone. If you have a partner, it means that you can never give up, because your partner is depending on you. On the days you think I am not doing enough and on the days I think you are not doing enough, even on those days we are still partners and we must not stop trying to finish the world. That's the deal." And they all agreed to the deal.

Then the angels asked God, "Is the world finished yet?" And God answered, "I don't know. Go ask my partners."[17]

This story affected me very strongly. And after many readings it still gets to me. I get tears in my eyes and choke up when I read the last line aloud. But this story is far from schmaltz. It is not a *Readers Digest* story designed to tug at one's heartstrings. It is a story that affects me because it changes the way I imagine things to be.

Like the creation stories in the book of Genesis, this story is a myth. The fact that it is obviously a myth bumps my modern, rational mind off questions about its factual nature. Like many people today, I have a hard time seeing Genesis as anything other than a naive, historically inaccurate fable. Because it isn't true (factual), it must be untrue (non-factual). So even though I know (rationally) that the story is a myth—"a story about realities whose truth is so profound that only a story can begin to capture it"[18] —I have great difficulty seeing it as a meaning-making myth. Gellman's

17. Marc Gellman, *Does God Have a Big Toe?: Stories about Stories in the Bible,* with paintings by Oscar de Mejo (New York: Harper & Row, 1989), 2–3. Used by permission.

18. Dreyer, *Earth Crammed with Heaven,* 68.

retelling recaptures the mythical nature of the story for me and allows it to evoke the truth that was intended.

Through the fanciful image of God creating order out of disorder amid a bunch of grumpy angels I was able to see God at play doing what God does, creating and ordering the universe. Exactly how God did it and continues to do it seems irrelevant now. Furthermore, the image of a partnership between God and us in the continuing work of creation jolted me out of my old image of the world as a something God created and then handed off to us to live in and use (in a moral and socially-conscious way, of course). But if God's work of creation isn't finished, and if we are God's partners, then our collective purpose as humans and my individual role in that purpose becomes much clearer.

The truth and meaning we draw from stories and images depends on who we are and where we are, of course. Images that affect me strongly will not necessarily affect someone else in the same way. Even so, some images, symbols, and stories have more power than others do, and that is why they are told and retold. By bearing clear images of truth, they elicit profound harmonics in many people and create a new sense of reality that conflicts with and undermines the old. Our after-the-fact efforts to talk about the truth we see suddenly are inadequate ways to capture the truth itself, but they are the basis of what has been called *theologia prima*—theology being born through the experience of God.[19]

YOU HAVE HEARD IT SAID . . .

Comedy is about provocation. We are led along thinking we know where the comedian is going, and then there is a juxtaposition of thought. Suddenly we see the situation from a different perspective. Jokes show us the absurdities of everyday life, in things that we take for granted—shopping, driving our cars, waiting in lines. What makes us laugh out loud is when suddenly we see these mundane things differently—when we are jolted into a new awareness. We get the joke and often the joke is on us.

Sometimes the jolt, the provocation, doesn't make us laugh. It makes us cry, shout, and think, "yes, now I get it" (or "how could I have been so stupid"), because what we see isn't absurd, it is freeing and enlightening (or shocking and disturbing). We have a new image that transforms our

---

19. Kavanagh, *On Liturgical Theology*, 74.

old way of seeing. Deliberate provocations in sermons include exaggerations, reversals of thought, distortions, outrageous statements, and impossibilities. One of Jesus' most shocking proverbs reads, "leave the dead to bury their own dead." Not as extreme, but still quite provocative is De Mello's suggestion that "One reason you join a religious organization is the chance it offers you to dodge religion with a clear conscience." And Brian Andreas offers this story: "The plumber was digging around in the pipes and he saw something shine in the muck and it turned out to be the lost soul of the last tenant. He gave it to me and I said I wonder how we can return it and he shrugged and said he found stuff like that all the time. You'd be amazed what people lose."[20]

Am I dead? What should I bury? Is my religion a way to dodge God? What have *I* lost lately? A sermon can jolt us out of our conceptual/perceptual ruts so that we can reexamine our unexamined assumptions about life. But the images we offer do not have to be shocking in order to engage and maintain the cycle of transformation. They must, however, seed our imaginations with images that evoke new associations.

All humans have "logic bubbles" or "thought worlds" that constrain how they see and experience reality.[21] We think inside the box, and we can't think outside the box because we are inside its walls. It is reality for us. As Edward de Bono notes, "we are very happy with what we have because we cannot conceive of anything better—and until we conceive of something better we are not motivated to look for it."[22] As sons and daughters of the Enlightenment, we see life in terms of cause-and-effect. As sons and daughters of God, we ought to see life in terms of advent and incarnation. Life is not causal; it is generative. Judgment has come and the verdict is salvation.

We can't fix misperceptions, but we can provoke disconnections, evoke new perceptions, and cook and stir the pot of change (in our congregations and the world). The words we use in our sermons are wild cards that provoke and evoke. For instance, in a sermon on Jeremiah 31: 33–34, Robert Marrone used the image of a carbon copy for a faith that is not our own—one that has been passed down from person to person, copied, and recop-

20. Luke 9:60 (NRSV); de Mello, *One Minute Nonsense*, 104; Brian Andreas, "The Plumber," *Story People* (Decorah, Ia.: StoryPeople, 1997), n.p.

21. See Eviatar Zerubavel, *Social Mindscapes: An Invitation to Cognitive Sociology* (Cambridge: Harvard University Press, 1997).

22. Edward de Bono, *de Bono's Thinking Course* (New York: Facts on File, 1994), 27.

ied. It is fuzzy; it is hard to read. And all the typing mistakes stand out. The lectionary reading states, "I will put my law within them, and I will write it on their hearts; and I will be their God, and they shall be my people. No longer shall they teach one another, or say to each other, 'know the Lord,' for they shall all know me. . . ." We don't need a copy. We can have the original. Marrone concluded by saying, "Technology tells us carbon copies are obsolete. Scripture tells us they are no longer necessary."

A sermon by Morgan Roberts titled "Are There Horses in Heaven?" began with the question asked by a child grieving over the death of her pet. From the image of dogs, cats, and horses in heaven, Roberts shifts to two provocative questions: "Will Jesus be in your heaven?" and "are your enemies in your heaven?" He says that for most of us heaven is like an ultimate vacation where good people (like us) receive rest and rewards. Would the Jesus of the New Testament be at home there? Would it be heaven for us unless our enemies were in some kind of hell? Well, are there horses in heaven? This is his answer: "Finding a place for a horse in heaven is not a problem for God. His Kingdom is very roomy. God can find room for another horse as easily as he can find room in his love for your worst enemy. So you can bring your horse or dog or cat, as long as you bring your enemy."[23]

These two sermons were about images, not answers. They did not tell the hearer what to do or how to live. Instead, they helped them see life from the perspective of God's Realm and "to draw from that experience their own way of life."[24]

ENTERING THE STREAM

Our illusions and delusions keep us from seeing and experiencing God's Kingdom—the reality of life in a realm that Jesus proclaimed as present and open to all. We cannot wish our delusions away or surgically remove them, either from ourselves or from our congregations. We can transform these illusions, however, and this is what a good sermon does. It begins with the false images that maintain our prisons and transforms them into new images that lead us into a new world.

---

23. F. Morgan Roberts, *Are There Horses in Heaven? and Other Thoughts: Sermons Preached in the Shadyside Presbyterian Church, Pittsburgh, Pennsylvania* (Pittsburgh: Lighthouse Point Press, 1996), 7.

24. Crossan, *In Parables*, 51.

A worship service should be transforming. A sermon should share in that transformational character. Yet no single service and no one sermon will transform anyone. Transformation is a process of flowering and fruiting, not for manufacturing transformed people. There are times when truth is sighted suddenly. A sermon may provide the catalyst for that transformation, but the process of getting to that moment of insight is as much a part of the transformational process as is the sudden sighting itself.

We help engage a cycle of transformation that people enter as they will. As the cycle continues, a motley collection of congregants is formed into an incarnational community with an integrity that is its own. It becomes one thing, an organism, but it is not like a bug or a tree or a person with a life cycle of birth, growth, and inevitable decline. A church is like a coral reef or an aspen grove—an organism that is a community of individuals—a thing that lives on through the renewing of its constituent parts.

To help engage a cycle of transformation within a congregation, we enter the cycle, exposing ourselves to ideas, images, and experiences that shake us out of the old and into new realities. When we experience the shattering of illusions and suddenly truth is sighted, it gives us something to say to people who are on the same path. According to Ludwig Wittgenstein, "The truth can be spoken only by someone who already lives inside it; not by someone who still lives in untruth and only sometimes reaches out from untruth toward it."[25]

The typical sermon is a laudable effort to educate, motivate, or alleviate. People have problems; we want to help. Fixing problems may work on cars, but it doesn't work on people. Life is problematic because our lives "don't fit into life's shape." When we change to fit that shape, "what is problematic disappears."[26] Transformation is all about that sort of change whereby we begin to fit life's shape. The minister aids in this process to the extent that she is being transformed and understands the illusions, hurts, and fears of her congregation. She weaves images and experiences that relate to where people live and offers them the possibility for something more, something real.

---

25. Excerpts from the writing of Ludwig Wittgenstein in *The Enlightened Mind: An Anthology of Sacred Prose*, ed. Stephen Mitchel (New York: HarperCollins, 1991), 200.

26. Ibid., 199.

Chapter eight

TRANSFORMING WORSHIP

Moving the national offices of the United Church of Christ from New York City to Cleveland in 1991 led to a lot of church shopping here on America's North Coast. Our staff fanned out across the city on Sunday morning visiting churches, trying to find new church homes. On Monday, we compared notes. "How was the service?" "Did you like the music?" "Did anyone actually speak to you after worship was over?" "That's an integrated area, were there any African Americans in the congregation?" "I heard that the minister there is very conservative, what did you think about his sermon?"

I rated the quality of each worship service that I attended and, as a sociologist who studies churches for a living, I probably was more critical than most people would be. I evaluate the style and quality of the music, the selection of hymns (can they be sung, are they relevant to the sermon, do they go together), the overall level of judgment and condemnation, the logic, point, and clarity of the message, the flow of the service, and the attention given to each worship element that is being performed. There is, of course, always something to criticize.

I am not alone in my tendency to evaluate worship. In fact, the Faith page of the Saturday London *Times* presents "At Your Service—A Five Star Guide," which reviews a different church/synagogue/mosque each week. Worship services are rated on: 1) the quality of the physical setting; 2) the quality of the sermon; 3) the spiritual "high"; 4) the quality of music; and 5) the quality of "after-service care." The *Times*'s Five Star Guide resembles a restaurant review, and perhaps that is appropriate because worship has become a commodity we evaluate based on the quality and quantity of the spiritual and temporal food it offers.

There is, of course, nothing wrong with enjoying worship, feeling better because of it, or learning something from the experience. It should not be something to be endured, despite what most five-year-old boys think. Worship is something we consume, but it also is something we create or bake ourselves. It is a communal process to which we jointly contribute and jointly benefit. It is a feast to which we bring our gifts, offer them to God, and see them returned to us, transformed, even as we are being formed into a community of transformed individuals.

I frequently use the wrong criteria to evaluate worship and I am not alone. In Cleveland, London, and all over the world, congregational audiences are evaluating the liturgical performances they see, and worship leaders are trying to make the experience more professional, more relevant, and more beneficial to an increasingly fickle public. This trend is not new. It is only more apparent today.

A SECULAR STRATEGY?

According to Alexander Schmemann, seeing the church as an outlet for the "bestowal of spiritual experience, spiritual food" is evidence of its secularization—not in the sense that the church has lost its "sacred quality," but that the church has accepted the functions that a secular society has relegated to it.[1] The primary functions of the church acting as a religious institution for secular society are 1) to *help individuals* alleviate their pain through a departure from the world into God's "transcendent Realm"; and 2) to *help society* maintain the civic order (and God's favor) through a strong moral code and sacred rituals. In the first function we see monasticism, Puritanism, sectarianism, evangelical efforts to save people out of the world, and contemplative efforts to retreat into the spiritual life. In the latter function, we see papal imperialism during the Middle Ages, Calvin's Geneva, Catholic Ireland, modern mainline efforts to make society more just, and efforts by the religious right to make society more moral.

Schmemann does not dispute the fact that the comfort-providing (opiate) and the societal support (status quo maintenance) functions are very useful and central to what any religion is expected to do. But that is his point. *Any* religion could perform these functions, so what then is the purpose of *Christianity*? Is it to perform those functions better than Judaism or Roman paganism?[2] No. The purpose of Christianity is to overcome the dualism (between the secular and the sacred) that makes the dual religious

---

1. Alexander Schmemann, *For the Life of the World: Sacrament and Orthodoxy* (Crestwood, N.Y.: St. Vladimir's Seminary Press, 1973), 12–13.

2. See Schmemann, *Introduction to Liturgical Theology*, trans. Asheleigh E. Moorhouse (Crestwood, N.Y.: St. Vladimir's Seminary Press, 1966), 30–31, 137–39.

functions necessary. Christianity is a way of liberation from a bondage that seeks to co-opt religion in order to keep people enslaved. It is not a once-a-week pass from our imprisonment (into God's Realm) nor is it a way to make our collective prisons better places to live.

In earlier eras, when people accepted the necessity of the church as the mediator between them and God, it was much easier for Christianity to perform its "religious" functions. An evangelical church actually did evangelism (rather than just talking about it), and political leaders saw the church as equal with the state. Those days are long gone in most of North America, and even in religious places like Quebec, Utah, and the Deep South, their days are numbered.

In order to keep people coming to our churches, we must *help them* in some way. We must provide valuable religious goods to church-shopping consumers. We must alleviate their pain. "Life in modern society is hard, so come to church so you will feel better" is the message, or "Recharge your spiritual batteries and then go back out into the world for another draining week."

Once we get people into the church, we must educate and reform them. Here, the legacy of medieval pietism rears its head and we begin the never-ending job of fixing what's wrong with people. And once people begin to be educated and indoctrinated into the ethic and ethos of the church, they can be motivated and persuaded to work on the goals of the church. They can be sent out to draw more people in, they can be sent out to reform the world, or they can stay inside and serve on more committees.

Worship, as the primary program of the church, reflects the operative purposes of the church to *alleviate*, *educate*, or *motivate*. The church as club or clan specializes in the first. The church as company or corporation emphasizes the second. The church as charismatic-leader-and-followers goes with the third. The church as incarnational community recognizes that its purpose is not to alleviate, educate, or motivate. Rather, its purpose is to *liberate*.

TO PROVOKE, EVOKE, AND TRANSFORM

We don't actually worship God. God does not require that we bow down and worship him.[3] Instead, what we do in our worship is communion with

---

3. My use of the masculine pronoun for God here is intentional and consistent with this incorrect image of a deity that demands our worship and supplication.

God in Christ as God's people. The purpose of worship is to come together as God's people, as the body of Christ, and be what we already are in praise of God's glory and celebration of what God has done. What worship does is to let us practice being what we are, seeing the world as God sees it—recognizing and realizing the Realm of God in our midst. Through such practice the community is formed, and we as individuals are transformed into members of it.

Attracting people to a religious performance and offering them Bible-based tips about how to live more fully will not result in lasting change in individual lives. Telling people about the needs of the world will not result in much justice-oriented action. In order to act differently, people must be changed fully, and this is a matter of transformation rather than accumulation. People are only transformed when their settled worlds are exploded and they participate bodily in experiences that place them inside a different reality. Worship disrupts our old way of seeing and thus allows movement into a new way of being. It provokes discomfort rather than alleviating it.[4]

Worship is sacramental in that it is passage from one state of being into another using the material world as a vehicle. In our physical assembling, we become the people of God, not to retreat together into a more spiritual place with God on the mountaintop, but to participate more fully in the world as it really is. According to Schmemann, "It is not an escape from the world, rather it is the arrival at a vantage point from which we can see more deeply into the reality of the world. The journey is to the Kingdom. This is where we are going—and not symbolically, but really."[5] Worship evokes a reality into which we can move.

Christian worship not only *says* something; it also *does* things. It shares this feature with other ritual expressions. According to Christopher Crocker, "Ritual . . . changes one season into another, makes boys become men, transforms ill persons into healthy ones and the ghosts of the dead into the souls of the ancestors."[6] Christian worship transforms us ritually into the body

---

4. The church certainly provides comfort and help for those hurting and in need. It is a loving community and responds to human hurts. The purpose of worship, however, is not to escape from suffering, but to experience life as God intended it to be. The result may feel like comfort to us, but in this case comfort is the indirect rather than direct consequence of what we are doing in worship.

5. Schmemann, *For the Life of the World*, 27, 29.

6. Christopher Crocker, "Ritual and the Development of Social Structure: Liminality and Inversion," *The Roots of Ritual*, ed. James D. Shaughnessy (Grand Rapids, Mich.: Eerdmans, 1973), 47.

of Christ. We become Christ. We don't imitate Christ.[7] Our transformation into the body of Christ is for the church and thus for the world. It is not for us, individually. It is to form the church. It also begins (and continues) the process of personal transformation so that we will be able to live fully in God's Realm, to experience the world as it really is. In the words of Thomas Merton, "Life is simple. We are living in a world that is absolutely transparent, and God is shining through it all the time."[8] We have become spiritual persons, not in some vague New Age sense, but as a people who have dropped our delusions, who can see the enchanted nature of the world and participate in its creative unfolding.

In figure 7 we see that the purpose of worship is not to alleviate. It is not about relief. It is about a cure—a cure that may be painful.[9] The purpose of worship also is not education, or at least not in the modern didactic sense of the word.[10] As Aiden Kavanagh states, "the liturgy is never used for ulterior motives such as education. [It] exists not to educate but to seduce people into participating in common activity of the highest order, where one is freed to learn things which cannot be taught."[11]

Worship also is not about motivation—another ulterior motive that those of us who have an audience find hard to resist. Like alleviation and education, motivation may be employed for good purposes. Surely the church should be engaged in good deeds, so why not use worship to rally the troops? But that is not worship. That is something else. The motivation to do justice may flow out of the transformation that begins in worship, but worship itself is about the creation of the capacity to recognize what should be done. It does not use guilt, emotional appeals, or high-minded rhetoric to

---

7. Anthony de Mello, *Awareness: A de Mello Spirituality Conference in His Own Words*, ed. J. Francis Stroud (New York: Doubleday/Image Books, 1990), 96.

8. Quoted by Marcus Borg, *The God We Never Knew: Beyond Dogmatic Religion to a More Authentic Contemporary Faith* (San Francisco: HarperSanFrancisco, 1997), 47.

9. de Mello, *Awareness*, 6, adds, "People don't really want to be cured. What they want is relief; a cure is painful."

10. Parker J. Palmer notes in *To Know as We Are Known: Education As a Spiritual Journey* (San Francisco: HarperSanFrancisco, 1993), 43, "the root meaning of 'to educate' is 'to draw out' and that the teacher's task is not to fill the student with facts but to evoke the truth the student holds within." However, most of us think about education as giving someone information that they should be able to use. So I prefer the term *evoke* which Palmer uses in his explanation of what education should be.

11. Aidan Kavanagh, *Elements of Rite: A Handbook of Liturgical Style* (New York: Pueblo Publishing, 1982), 28.

move people in the direction that a minister thinks they should go. D‹
so changes worship and congregations into things that they are not.

Figure 7
ALTERNATIVE PURPOSES FOR WORSHIP

WAY OF THE WORLD (IN THE REALM OF DELUSION)	WAY OF CHRIST (IN THE REALM OF GOD)
To: Alleviate *or* Educate *or* Motivate	To: Provoke *and* Evoke *and* Transform

In worship we *provoke*, *evoke*, and *transform*. We use the subversive power of the Gospel to undermine safe assumptions. We sing songs, enter processions, and enact rituals that make us a people. We learn to see with different eyes and then go out into a transformed reality to continue God's creative work. We do not attend worship because God requires it of us as individuals. The church worships because that is what it does. We attend because the people of God are having a feast, and we don't want to miss it. But what if it is not a feast? What if it is not a setting where the church is realized? If it is something else, is there any reason to go? Perhaps not, other than the threat of retribution and the promise of a reward—preschool motivations that we cannot seem to outgrow.

THEOLOGY AND PRACTICALITY

All of this may not seem very practical. I understand that. When I presented some of the material in this chapter to the Executive Council of the United Church of Christ, one of the first questions I received was "What do you think our worship should look like?" I cannot answer that question except by referring to what worship is and does rather than to its style or use/non-use of certain worship resources, techniques, or procedures. Indeed, the major problem with worship stems from treating it as a performance containing resources, techniques, and procedures—things that must be updated and shifted around in order to plan a more pleasing order of service.

We do some things because they are traditional: Reformed churches have a long prayer of confession; Baptist churches have a long altar call; Episcopal churches use the Book of Common Prayer; Catholic churches use missalettes. Almost all churches include hymns, prayers for the people, an offering, a sermon, and a benediction. Most churches include a greeting, choral music, a pastoral prayer, and the Lord's Prayer. Some churches feature testimonies, weekly communion, censing the altar, speaking in tongues, kneeling, bowing, rock bands, liturgical dance, or uniformed nurses. A few churches stress silence, holy laughter, casting out demons, or the handling of snakes. Within specific worship traditions there is a limited range of possibilities. Churches may move things around within this range, but people become uncomfortable when foreign elements are imported from other traditions. So we try to construct a pleasing program using the building blocks that are available to us from our religious tradition and that are familiar to the members of our particular congregation. If we want to change things radically, the best we can do is to add an alternative service, such as contemporary worship on Saturday night or a contemplative chapel service early Sunday morning.

Making worship more attractive to religious consumers usually involves doing traditional things better—packaging them in a new way or making them more professional. Only new independent churches have the luxury of creating an order of worship from scratch and adding a lot of nontraditional elements such as skits, mime, interactive games, video clips, and PowerPoint presentations. But whether you are the minister or worship leader in a traditional church or a modern church in the Willow Creek megachurch mode, there are limits, and these limits are part of specific liturgical traditions that emerged centuries ago.

The typical mainline Protestant service *sans communion* is a historical artifact of infrequent communion of the late Middle Ages. The leaders of the Reformation wanted more frequent communion, not less of it, and certainly never intended for the Eucharist to be an addendum celebrated quarterly or only on Sunday evenings. The mainline also inherited the medieval predisposition toward a "heavily penitential, didactic, and disciplinary" service of the Word.[12]

The typical evangelical Protestant service developed out of frontier revival services and camp meetings, which were used in nineteenth century America to help churches catch up with a population that had spread westward, out of the reach of established congregations.[13] So even though we no longer have a large unevangelized population in North America, conservative churches (both electronic and real) persist in the frontier worship strategy: music to soften up the audience, a convicting sermon, and a call to respond (to be healed, saved, or to send in a check).

Protestant worship today seems to be determined more by a historical Catch-22 and the demographics of a developing nation than by theology, ideology, or purpose. Given this reality, what are mainline churches in North America to do about their worship? Are we to follow the lead of Roman Catholic churches (the ones who think the Second Vatican Council was a good thing) into liturgical renewal, or do we emulate the evangelicals and transform our worship into a mainline version of the frontier design?

Actually, we pursue neither strategy because the way we reform our worship must grow out of what we are doing now. Each church must allow its own incarnation to emerge out of its present practices, purposes, and theology of liturgy rather than by constructing a more pleasing worship experience through rational planning or the emulation of others. Worship should not be a mindless continuation of what we are doing now, but neither should it be a calculated construction of something that might be better.

---

12. James F. White, *Introduction to Christian Worship*, rev. ed. (Nashville, Tenn.: Abingdon Press, 1990), 155.

13. White, *Protestant Worship: Traditions in Transition* (Louisville, Ky.: Westminster/John Knox, 1989), 173.

GROWING YOUR OWN

Several years ago, a dying Roman Catholic parish in downtown Cleveland, Ohio, revamped both its sanctuary and worship service. Pews were torn out and replaced by rows of heavy oak chairs facing the center of the sanctuary. The white-painted interior, stone floor, and lighted candles in iron sconces on soaring columns create the sense of worship in a European abbey. There are no missalettes to follow. There are no hymnals. The worship bulletin contains the gathering hymn, responsorial psalm, and communion hymn. Sometimes the gathering hymn is a chant in Latin (*Domine, Domine . . .*). There is no real program or order of service because the liturgy does not require one. The service is initiatory. It simply flows, and even a first-time, non-Catholic visitor can step into the stream without any hesitation or confusion.

The Bible passages are read according to the lectionary and the pastor, Robert Marrone, gives a brief but very evocative homily. After monetary gifts are collected during the offering, the people bring gifts of wine and bread in a dramatic procession from the back of the church to the altar. The priest censes the altar and then the congregation. Most people bow. The smell of incense fills the sanctuary. It recalls the words of an oft-sung gathering hymn, "Let my prayer arise as incense in your sight. The lifting of my hands a sign of trust in you O God."

The "passing of the peace" marks the start of something unexpected. As people greet one another there is little chitchat because it is the beginning of a ritual of formation.[14] Greetings continue as the congregation moves from their seats to gather as the people of God in a circle around a large stone altar where Father Marrone sings the Eucharistic prayer as a dialogical litany with the congregation. After the breaking of the bread and blessing of the wine, the priest and the celebrants move back down to the center of the sanctuary. The congregation turns and follows, taking communion and returning to their seats for private prayer or to sing the communion hymn.

What kind of worship is this? Is it traditional or is it contemporary? It has been criticized for being too much of both. There actually is no word for what it is because it seems to be both traditional and contemporary simultaneously—without a jarring mixture of a traditional-bit followed

---

14. According to Robert Marrone (personal interview 1999), "the gathering around is for one simple fact, we're doing it, I'm not."

by a contemporary-bit. In describing the service, I call it *avant-garde ancient*. It is a style full of symbolism, ritual, tastes, smells, and meaning-filled words. The repetitive responses, the use of a flute during offertory, and the canter singing the communion hymn give much of the service a contemplative tone. There is silence but no dead time. No one is leafing through booklets to find a reading. No one gets bored or loses interest.

This church—St. Peter Church in Cleveland, Ohio—has created something unique, grounded in liturgical history, that fits its pastor and worshiping community. That creation changes slightly from year to year. There is no fanfare about the changes. New elements just seem to happen and the congregation goes with the flow even though the service is not quite the same. It is not necessary to explain or instruct the congregation during the Mass.

Whether a worship service is traditional, contemporary, or avant-garde ancient, it should always have integrity. That is, the parts of the worship service should join together in a coherent whole with the same purpose. Just as a church is not a collection of programs to be resourced, worship is not a program of performances to be completed. Robert Marrone says that liturgy is "fundamentally choreography," where we "experience symbols in their fullest form" in a seamless flow. It is something we co-create by bringing our bodies, our gifts, and our openness to God.

Worship in its present incarnation at St. Peter's was not the result of rational planning nor did it just happen. As with most things in life, it emerged through the synergy of the ingredients that were available, the resolute actions of the pastor and parishioners, the unfolding nature of their collective creation, and surprising events that led the church in new directions. What St. Peter's began with was a dead congregation in an empty, crumbling, nineteenth-century sanctuary, a priest who was a student of the liturgy, and a handful of eager students from Cleveland State University where the pastor also served as chaplain. At his first Mass, the pastor was greeted by a dozen long-time members all seated on the last two rows—over one-hundred feet from the pulpit. He walked down to where they all were and preached the homily from there. He also threatened to remove pews from the back unless they moved forward. After a few weeks of pew removal, they got the message. Soon after a chunk of stone fell off the church and rolled into the street. The building had to be renovated, a process that continues today.

One thing led to another, which led to another, and because the congregation was composed of elderly people who did not want their church to die and students who were willing to try anything, change occurred more rapidly than would have been possible in a relatively healthy parish.

All across North America, older churches are ripping out their immovable pews. New churches are designing worship spaces to facilitate movement and flexibility. They are heeding the words of liturgists like Kavanagh who said, "pews nail the assembly down, proclaiming that the liturgy is not a common action but a preachment perpetuated upon the seated, an ecclesiastical opera done by virtuosi for a paying audience. . . . Filling a church with immovable pews is similar to placing bleachers directly on a basketball court."[15] Charles Fulton, president of the Episcopal Church Building Fund is even more blunt. He tells Episcopal parish leaders considering a new or refurbished sanctuary that "pews are the work of the Devil."

Most Christians who sit in a fixed pew toward the rear of the sanctuary (or even at the front) have never thought about why their church should or should not have pews or theater seats.[16] They also have never considered why their church does a lot of other things it does in worship or how it got that way. A lot of clergy probably haven't worried about such things either.[17]

The point is, what we do in worship has an effect and that effect may be counter to what we intend and counter to the purpose of worship as we understand it. We change worship by attention to its purpose, our theology, the rich history of Christian liturgy, and the people who are in our congregation. Just as St. Peter's did, we begin with who we are as a congregation and as individuals, with the gifts God has given us and through resolute corporate action. We also begin with the problems—our own crumbling walls—and we use them as ingredients for the transformation of our worship and our church. Once we begin the process of change, we become the situation and the situation becomes us. It is impossible to put things back the way they were.

Because most of our churches are not dying and Protestant pastors do not have the authority that they think most Roman Catholic priests hold, we may not be able to change as rapidly as St. Peter Church. Nevertheless, most of us would rather begin the process of change with a relatively healthy

---

15. Kavanagh, *Elements of Rite*, 21–22.

16. Theater seats are increasingly common in large Baptist and other evangelical churches. They complete the image of the congregation as passive audience for professional performers.

17. One reason for the lack of concern is the minimal attention given to such practical matters in most Protestant seminaries. Thankfully, this situation seems to be changing with regard to worship.

congregation, rather than one that must change or die. Either way, healthy or sick, we must start from where we are. Some heavy pruning back may be necessary, but in any church there is healthy rootstock to begin the process of renewal and growth.

WORSHIPING ON PURPOSE

Worship is not a performance put on by professionals for paying parishioners, but it is a drama in which we all play parts, acting out our roles and drawing our own meaning, understanding, and emotion. Through choreographed action, scripted words, and music to express meanings too real to be read, we recreate the reality of which our symbols speak.

The only way for worship to do what it is supposed to do (form us into a people of transformed individuals who see the world as God sees it) is through symbols and song, images and the imagination. "Some things cannot be said," at least not through words which try to tell the truth.[18] But words can *evoke* the truth that we might otherwise try to capture in concepts. Any truth that can be captured is not the truth of God—"It is only through the ambiguity of symbol that the meaning can be experienced. Efforts to pin it down transform it into something that it is not."[19]

Symbolic words, rituals, parables, stories, metaphors, and myths are essential if worship is to have the power to transform rather than reform, if it is to liberate rather than reiterate. Symbols "coax one into a swamp of meaning and require one to frolic in it," as Kavanagh says.[20] When we crawl out of that swamp, we are covered in meaningful muck. We know what the truth is, what it feels like all over and inside.

The problem is that most rational-minded North Americans see symbols as distracting and rituals as empty. We participate in them, but we do not get their meaning. To overcome the disconnection between symbols and their meaning, we are tempted to explain them as we conduct the ritual. We hold up the bread of the Eucharist and say "this is what it symbolizes." At weddings, we hold up the ring and talk about how it forms an endless circle of love. We kill ritual with commentary. Nevertheless, the logic of ritual assumes that people recognize the meaning of symbols so the "mean-

---

18. Kavanagh, *Elements of Rite*, 102.
19. Kavanagh, *On Liturgical Theology* (New York: Pueblo Publishing, 1984), 98.
20. Kavanagh, *Elements of Rite*, 5.

ing packets" that comprise the ritual can be invoked and burst open in people's minds while they are participating. Instruction is essential to the maintenance of meaning, but not during the rite itself.

In the Eucharist, when the bread is placed in our hands, the minister, celebrant, priest, or our fellow congregant says to us, "The body of Christ." What those symbolic words are intended to evoke is the awareness that we are taking the body of Christ into our bodies and we are becoming it. It doesn't become part of us. We become part of it. The priest does not explain that meaning, however. We are supposed to know it and thus experience once again the mystery of becoming Christ. It is not his sacrifice apart from us. It is our sacrifice too. We are standing before God as Christ in the Eschaton, beyond time and space, and can say along with St. John Chrysostom, "but what do I care about heaven, when I myself have become heaven."[21]

Music is another largely non-rational element of worship.[22] It helps remove distractions and focuses our attention on what we are doing. It is not an escape, but a means of concentrating the rhythmic efforts of the congregational "work crew" on their job, the liturgy—the work of the people. The power of the gospel as preached by the pastor provokes openness to new awareness. Songs well-up memories, evoke images, and create a sense of unity. We are celebrating this feast together. Music and ritual, rich with symbol, evoke a sense of who we are as a people, the presence of God in our midst, and the sacred nature of the world.

Creating or baking a worship service that does what it is supposed to do must follow the organic logic of God's Realm rather than the ascetic, pietistic logic of the Middle Ages. It also should not follow the educational, humanistic logic of the Enlightenment or the recreational, dilettante logic of postmodern North America. Our goal is not to please God, reform repeat offenders, gather a moral community, or captivate an audience. There is no clear, idealistic outcome to be achieved. Liturgy "leads not to the brink of clarity but to the edge of chaos. It deals not with the abolition of ambiguity but with the dark and hidden things of God."[23]

---

21. Schmemann, *For the Life of the World*, 37.

22. This section was aided greatly by the comments of Judith Bullock in a lecture and workshop on music and liturgy. She is director of worship for the Archdiocese of Louisville, Kentucky.

23. Kavanagh, *Elements of Rite*, 102.

The purpose of right worship, *orthodoxia*, is to reset the secular system and transform it into a system with a logic of its own.[24] We do not want to alleviate, educate, or motivate. We want to *cultivate, generate*, and *incarnate*. That is, we want to put into play a transforming, generative, incarnational system, and worship helps do that by disrupting the old secular system. Worship allows us to imagine a new way of being and helps us move into it by practicing the principles of cultivation, generation, and incarnation.

CAN THIS SERVICE BE SAVED?

Most people who will read this book conduct worship services without a weekly communion and without a lot of other rituals and symbols. Is it possible to transform traditional Protestant worship without adopting a form of worship that people will find foreign? Yes, because I am not saying that the answer to our worship problem is to be found in reverting to the historic worship pattern of Synaxis (liturgy of the Word) followed by Eucharist. If it were as simple as that, the typical Roman Catholic service would not be so grim.

St. Peter Church provides an illustration of how Catholic worship can be redeemed. It also provides an illustration of how certain universal worship principles work. A worship service should *flow*; moving from exciting highs to contemplative lows in a series of undulating waves. Worship should engage the congregation in *communal action*, over and over, so that the service helps to form the Christian community. Disparate individuals are transformed into a people acting together. The sermon or homily should be an integral part of the service, one of the highs rather than a low. It should provoke a disruption of unexamined assumptions rather than reinforcing what everyone already believes.

African American churches also provide an example of how worship can flow seamlessly and how a congregation is formed into an active, participating community. Sitting passively in pews is hardly possible. Hymns pull the congregation into a unified whole, praising God together. Sermons are not educational; they are symbolic and highly ritualistic. They use story,

---

24. See Kavanagh, *On Liturgical Theology*, 81–82. He maintains that the term Orthodoxia, right worship, has been mistranslated and misconstrued into meaning "right believing." This change in meaning reflects a divergence between praxis and belief and the primacy of doctrine over our encounter with God, according to Kavanagh.

drama, rhythmic repetition, and a running dialogue with the congregation. The sermon is not a lecture. It is a microcosm of the entire worship service. It provokes, evokes, and unifies.

We can learn something about the choreography of worship from both Catholic and black Protestant churches. One thing we learn is that worship should have a flow—it should be a single thing that we break open and let what's inside gush out. The second thing we learn is that worship should draw us together; it should form us into a people, a community, rather than fostering our separation as individual, isolated worshipers. It is not possible to worship as an individual aesthete, appreciating the performance while sitting in a pew. You can exercise devotional piety that way, but you can't worship. The third thing we learn is that worship must involve ritual and symbol. Through ritual and the symbolic meaning packets it contains, we are transformed. People cannot be argued into the Kingdom. As the Realm of truth, it must be sighted suddenly and will only be recognized from within. Anglican, Catholic, Orthodox, African American, Pentecostal, and even some Quaker churches rely heavily on ritual to evoke the presence of God among us and the sense that we are present to God, in Christ.

Less is more. A clean, simple service—in which carefully chosen symbol and song stand out—communicates a message that speaks volumes. White Protestant churches seem to believe that more is more, but when a minister actually speaks in volumes, people miss the message. Our transformational purpose should be our guide, rather than the need to get it all in.

There is no reason to begin worship with three disparate songs in a row. There is no need for penitential prayers that contradict the preacher. There is no need for a long pastoral prayer that previews the sermon. There is no need to hold three or four books on one's lap in order to keep up with the action. There is no need for long readings that lull a congregation to sleep. My advice is to replace half of your explanation with imagination. Even with that loss, you will be left with plenty.

What we want to grow and nurture is a service where everything is done on purpose for a purpose. The service should draw the community together, focus its attention, point to God's reality, evoke an awareness of God's presence, and give praise and glory to God for what God has done. All of that can be done through music, song, participatory ritual, the prayers of the people, statements of faith, and a sermon that uses scripture to undermine assumptions.

Growing a worship service that seeks to transform rather than reform typically involves elimination of the accumulation. Why are we doing what we are doing? What is the implicit or explicit theology behind it? Does it contribute to or detract from our purpose? We ask these questions and then we can move to alternatives. What can we learn from Christian history? How did the church worship prior to becoming the state religion of a secular empire? What can we learn from the renewal of liturgy in the Catholic church and in all mainline Protestant denominations? What new rituals are emerging among innovative, purposeful churches?[25]

Each worship service provides an opportunity for doing things slightly different. Major changes done hastily only create confusion, and worship by its very nature must change slowly. New directions and alterations that don't work should be discarded. Helpful new directions can be followed to see where they lead. A clear purpose, a sound theology of worship, and the response of the people provide the needed editing tools to decide what we will do this week, and the next.

---

25. Examples I have observed include a one-time ritual in a UCC church and a ritual that is repeated regularly in many Unitarian Universalist churches. The first occurred during worship a few years ago at Federated Church in Chagrin Falls, Ohio. A group of children collected money for hunger relief in the community and wanted to show the congregation what they had done. They could have announced the amount of money collected. Instead, they did something that was both concrete and symbolic. The children went next door to a grocery store and were given lists of food to put in their carts. The money they collected went to pay for the food. After filling the carts, the children wheeled them from the store up the street to the church and pushed them into the sanctuary—ringing the congregation with shopping carts brimming with food. It was a new ritual: a clear, symbolic demonstration by these children of their hard work and commitment to provide food for the needy persons living in their community.

An ongoing rite in many Unitarian Universalist congregations is the ritual of the candle. In this ceremony, which generally takes place early in the worship service, members of the congregation are invited to come to the front of the sanctuary, light a candle, and share something that is on their heart to the congregation—a joy, a sadness, a word of hope. At a service I attended in Boston, a woman talked about the death of her cat and how the vet she took it to when it became sick didn't seem to understand what the cat meant to her. After all, it was an old cat. So they let it die, and now she misses her cat very much. Most of the congregation was in tears after she finished, including me. A man told about his partner who recently died of AIDS. But not all of the messages were sad. A woman talked about reconciling with her family after many years of estrangement. A young man talked about his excitement about a new job. This ritual—more than any solicitation of prayer requests—gave permission and a place set apart for people to share joys and sorrows. According to Larry Peers, a Unitarian Universalist leader, it was a ritual of openness that allowed people to cut through the superficialities of everyday communication and help form a beloved community, present to each other.

Chapter nine

FORMATION AND TRANSFORMATION IN A COMMUNITY OF FAITH

You have to remember to make it over again every day. . . .
Otherwise it all goes to Hell."

—Brian Andreas[1]

I WAS VERY GOOD at math when I was growing up. In high school I loved to solve algebra problems, and in college I found calculus to be just as easy. Today, I can still add and subtract, multiply and divide, but algebra and calculus are beyond me. I look at the formulas and can't remember what to do. The knowledge I once held slipped away. I forgot it before my senior year in college.

I was reared in the Bible Belt during the religious fifties. Not surprisingly, my family went to church and Sunday school every week. I heard a lot about the Bible during those years, but my most vivid memories of Sunday school are of sitting in the back row of the classroom with my friends whispering about the latest episode of Gunsmoke. I learned a moral code and some basic facts about the Bible—the adding and subtracting of Christianity—but I didn't retain much else.[2]

A few other childhood learning experiences were much more vivid and long-lasting. I remember one Christmas morning Santa Claus brought our family a unicycle, but no one knew how to ride it. So my brother, sister, and several cousins spent the better part of a week in Gulfport, Mississippi, practicing the way that seemed most logical to us—mounting the unicycle while bracing one arm against our parent's station wagon, pedaling alongside the

---

1. Brian Andreas, "Remembering" *Story People* (Decorah, Ia.: StoryPeople, 1997), n.p.

2. My religious imagination remained alive to some extent from my mother reading from a Bible storybook and through the full set of *Oz* books.

car, and then trying to keep going. It was a very inefficient learning strategy that resulted in many bloody ankles and skinned knees. What we didn't realize was that riding a unicycle is not like riding a bicycle. Speed does not increase stability. Unicycles are all about being able to balance over one spot. If you can balance without moving, it is relatively easy to move forward and keep going. Without anyone to demonstrate this skill, or to tell us what we were doing wrong, we kept at our trial and error method—riding and crashing, riding and crashing.

After about five days of constant failure, one by one we began to get the balance. And once you get it, you really get it. I went fifteen wobbly feet before falling. On my next turn I went two blocks. After that I could ride as long as I wanted. I never forgot how to do it. No matter how many years go by without riding a unicycle, I can still get right on and not fall off. The skill is in my bones.

I would suggest that learning the way of Christ is an experience that is much more akin to learning to ride a unicycle than it is to learning about the Bible in Sunday school. It is as much about the body as the mind.[3] We learn it by the full-bodied experience of doing it and allowing it to become part of our being.

FORMATION IS FOR CHILDREN; TRANSFORMATION IS FOR ADULTS

Children are naturally religious. They see mystery and magic all around them and must be taught to see the way adults see—that is to separate reality from make-believe. It is not possible to convert young children. They are already in God's Realm. Adults, on the other hand, cannot see over the walls of culturally-created ruts into the Realm in which children play. Adults require what Aidan Kavanagh calls "conversion therapy" to restore their awareness of God—to poke open their "inward eyes" so they can see fully once again.[4]

We get it backwards. We treat adults as if they need to be formed and children as if they need to be transformed. Formation is for children and its

---

3. The dualism of the body versus the mind is artificial, of course. That is the point.

4. Aidan Kavanagh, *On Liturgical Theology* (New York: Pueblo Publishing, 1984), 167. The term "inward eyes" is from Ephesians 1:18. It is sometimes translated as "the eyes of your heart" (NRSV).

purpose is not to produce knowledgeable adults.[5] Its purpose is to practice using the inward eye—to keep their whole sight open—and thus eliminate the necessity for conversion therapy later in life.[6] Christian formation is a subversive process that keeps children connected to God's Realm and thus aware of the ultimate unreality of a social order that wants them to live, think, and see according to its rut-bound rules. The church helps form an awareness of what is real and what is really only pretend.

Yet we want to convert our children. Why? Because Christianity began as a religion that converted adults—as evidenced by the once-central rite of baptism. So we treat children as if they were little adults. When they are old enough to understand God, we teach our children Christian answers to adult questions and then expect them to decide in favor of what they have been taught. Evangelical churches even expect the decision to be an emotional one—to be an adult-like conversion in which a six-year-old child turns away from her presumably sinful life and makes a decision for Christ.

Confirmation occurs later—after the child has been conditioned by society—and attempts to re-form the teenager through the usual pedagogical technique of information providing.[7] Paulo Freire calls this the "banking approach" to education, whereby the teacher fills students by "making deposits of information."[8] By knowing the faith intellectually, the teen is then accepted into full church membership. It is not (usually) a rite of passage—a mini-transformation—which ritually initiates the youth into a new role, that of a responsible adult member in the Christian community.

Jesus said, "Let the little children come to me, and do not stop them; for it is to such as these that the kingdom of heaven belongs."[9] Children already see Jesus. The kingdom of heaven already belongs to them. We should keep the path open and not block their way. Christian formation is all about that process—keeping open the path to Jesus and life in God's Realm and not putting up barriers to it.

---

5. See Jack Mezirow, *Transformative Dimensions of Adult Learning* (San Francisco: Jossey-Bass, 1991), 3.

6. Or more likely, to make the process of adult conversion more natural, like rediscovering a foreign language that you learned as a child.

7. James F. White calls confirmation "a practice looking for a theology." *Introduction to Christian Worship*, rev. ed. (Nashville, Tenn.: Abingdon, 1990), 211.

8. Paulo Freire, "Pedagogy of the Oppressed," *The Paulo Freire Reader*, ed. Ana Maria Araújo Freire and Donaldo Macedo (New York: Continuum, 1998), 70–71.

9. *New Revised Standard Version.*

Christian formation is a type of socialization. But it is socialization of a peculiar sort, which seeks to maintain a child's sense of wonder and comfort with mystery and myth, rather than killing them through reason and the weight of adult information. Formation occurs primarily through the telling of stories, the engagement of the religious imagination, and role play.[10] By participating in the rich symbolic life of the church as children, when their religious imaginations are fully alive, the rituals and stories of the church are infused with meaning that can be evoked or triggered throughout their lives. The meaning will be in their bones and thus "re-membered" over and over.

Sophia Cavalletti describes the process through which a child "falls in love with God" and perceives "the religious content of reality in its wholeness" as learning "the key to creation."[11] Without that key to interpret reality, the inherent wonder and unity of God's Realm will be lost to meaningless descriptions of what things "are." The critical years are early when "everything is a source of wonder because everything is new."[12] The parables provide a rich way to begin.

For example, Cavalletti uses the parable of the mustard seed to engage the child's sense of wonder. She says: "What extraordinary energy there must be to transform the little seed into a tree, or into a full ear of grain, or a small handful of flour and water into a swollen lump of dough! Would we know how to do it ourselves? Is there any person who can do such a thing?" The children respond to her questions. She helps them recognize the same energy in their bodies. "We were so small when we were born! Now look at us! How tall are we? How long are our arms, our legs? Is it due to us? If I wanted to grow taller or shorter, could I do it?" She talks with the children about the changes that are happening to them and says that even when their bodies stop growing physically they still have the capacity to become greater. A child named Linda exclaims, "A kingdom inside us!"

---

10. See Sonja M. Stewart and Jerome W. Berryman, *Young Children and Worship* (Louisville, Ky.: Westminster/John Knox, 1989) for helpful information about how to engage children in worship and ritual role play.

11. Sophia Cavalletti, *The Religious Potential of the Child: Experiencing Scripture and Liturgy with Young Children*, trans. Patricia M. Coulter and Julie M. Coulter (Chicago: Liturgy Training Publication, 1992), 143.

12. Ibid., 138.

In another example, Cavalletti presents the parable of the leaven by helping children prepare bread dough and watch it rise in the pan. And what do the children say? "It's so big!" "It's true! Jesus was right! Jesus tells the truth."

Teaching children through role-play, or as Gabriel Moran says, "by showing how," yields unexpected rewards.[13] One Sunday earlier this year, a four-year-old girl tugged on Father Marrone's sleeve after Mass and said to him, "you're wearing green—that's ordinary time!" How did she know that and why did she want to tell him? She learned about liturgical colors by role-playing worship, Montessori style. She wanted to tell him because the green on his robe held meaning for her. The green wasn't just green anymore, nor did it merely stand for something else. To a child or to an adult with a religious imagination, the green *is* "ordinary time." By "doing it" and combining doing with stories about what they were doing, the children learned worship and symbols in a way that eludes adults.[14] Just as children learn languages much more easily than adults do, children also learn easily the symbols, myths, and rituals of the church—the language and culture of spirituality. This is important, because as Wittgenstein says, "*The limits of my language* mean the limits of my world."[15] To expand our worlds, we must expand our language. But without the opportunity to go back and relearn what we missed when we could learn it best, the church must provide Rosetta Stones to help interpret the unfamiliar writing of the Realm.

08

A CYCLE OF TRANSFORMATION

Adults—and particularly adults in modern Western society—are not naturally religious. Reality is in the here and now—what we can see, feel, and name. We are empirical existentialists who have a great problem seeing the point of myth, symbol, and mystery. We don't want wonder in our religion (or to wonder about our religion).

---

13. Gabriel Moran, *Showing How: The Act of Teaching* (Valley Forge, Penn.: Trinity, 1997).

14. For more information about this style of religious education for children, see Jerome W. Berryman's books, *Godly Play: A Way of Religious Education* (San Francisco: HarperSanFrancisco, 1991) and *Teaching Godly Play: The Sunday Morning Handbook* (Nashville, Tenn.: Abingdon Press, 1995).

15. Ludwig Wittgenstein, *Tractatus Logico-Philosophicus* (Mineola, N.Y.: Dover, 1922), 88 [5.6].

We must be transformed into people whose eyes are open to the signs of God's kingdom. Transformation is a magical process, but it does not happen all at once through the wave of a wand, a trip down an aisle, or the praying of a prayer. We move from insight to understanding to a new incarnation, as a new way of seeing becomes a new way of being. The process is continuous. We are not transformed from one thing into another thing that is better. We do not become ideal Christians or Christians seeking an ideal. Instead, we enter into a cycle of continuous transformation as the light of God and the sustaining ground of a Christian community allow us to grow, develop, and bear fruit.

The problem, of course, is that people don't want to be transformed or don't see the necessity. Whether the old system is working for us or not, it is our world, and from the inside we cannot see it for what it is.[16] We must be jolted out of the old and into the new. Walter Brueggemann describes the initial process as a "movement" of disorientation, loss of control, and emptying. He suggests that such a change is a "necessary precondition of new life."[17]

The word *insight* is used for the initial stage of transformation in figure 8 below. It is here that we DWJD (Do What Jesus Did): Provoke a disconnection with the old and evoke an awareness of the new. We plant seeds of meaning that germinate and grow in the space cleared by verbal "hand grenades."

As discussed in the previous two chapters, the primary locus of liberation is worship and the primary source of provocation is the sermon or homily. It is here that we begin to reset the system by using images that are inconsistent with thinking and perception in our old worlds. Like the electric paddles that emergency room doctors use to restart hearts, words can be used to shock open our inward eyes. For instance, Jesus tells us that it is easier for a camel to go through the eye of a needle than for a rich man to enter the Kingdom of God. Annie Dillard says, "God does not direct the universe, he underlies it."[18] Ludwig Wittgenstein observes that "Death is

---

16. According to Wittgenstein, *Tractatus Logico-Philosophicus*, 105, "The sense of the world must lie outside the world. In the world everything is as it is and happens as it does." We take it for granted because we are in it.

17. Walter Brueggemann, *The Message of the Psalms: A Theological Commentary* (Minneapolis: Augsburg, 1984), 11.

18. Annie Dillard, *For the Time Being* (New York: Knopf, 1999), 140.

Figure 8

A TRANSFORMATIONAL PROCESS

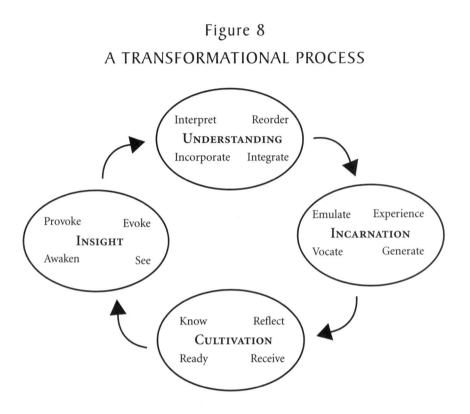

not an event of life."[19] Robert Marrone once said in a homily at St. Peter Church, "It is not necessary to love God, nor is it possible." The truth communicated by these statements is less in their literal interpretation than in their ability to disconnect us from old patterns of thought. They may shock us, anger us, confuse us, or make us say, "that's not right!" But that's the point. That's also the point of this entire book.

The way provocations work is described at great length by Edward de Bono. He says that humans form perceptual patterns that help us live, but restrict our ability to see anything new. Provocations force us out of these perceptual patterns and allow us to change through the formation of new patterns that we connect back existing channels of thought. Provocations come at us by accident sometimes (leading to most of the world's inventions) or through disasters, but they can also be invoked intentionally. De

---

19. Wittgenstein, *Tractatus Logico-Philosophicus* , 106.

Bono says that one way to create such intentional provocations is through the use of "random words."[20]

As a test of de Bono's idea, I used the random word procedure in this book to help develop several new metaphors. First, I thought of a problem that I wanted to think about differently. I then looked up a word in my dictionary by opening the book to a random page and placing my finger on a word without looking. I then tried to imagine how that randomly selected word might be related to the problem I identified. It sounds crazy, but it worked. The reason it worked is that a word that has nothing to do with your problem forces you outside your existing channels of thinking, thus enabling you to see the problem in a different way.

The problems or processes I identified were worship, Christian education, stewardship, religious practices, and evangelism. The respective wild card words I found were these: carbon cycle, carrot, punch card, cowpatty, and ketogenesis. Believe it or not I was able to make useful connections between all of these words and the church-related concepts.

For instance, the dictionary definition for "carbon cycle"—the word I found for worship—mentioned two processes of transformation. One occurs in the sun as atoms are combined to create energy through nuclear fusion. The other is photosynthesis—the process through which plants grow by using sunlight to break down carbon dioxide into its constituent elements. Not only did the wild card technique give me a new metaphor for worship (a type of fusion reaction); it also helped break up my rut of thinking about transformation as a disruptive process with a discrete end. In fusion and photosynthesis, the transformation (bringing things together and creating something new) is a continuous process. It is a natural, ongoing cycle.

We provoke in order to disrupt old patterns of thinking and to allow the creation of new, life-giving ways of seeing and being. The goal is not simply to create mental chaos. When we provoke, we also evoke an awareness of a transformed reality. We also model that reality through worship, so the evocation is doubly powerful. When our vision clears and a new path emerges, the reality we envision is before us. We are liberated from the old and able to move into the new.

---

20. See Edward de Bono, *de Bono's Thinking Course*, rev. ed. (New York: Facts on File, 1994) and *I am Right, You are Wrong: From This to the New Renaissance, from Rock Logic to Water Logic* (London: Viking, 1990).

UNDERSTANDING

Insight only begins the process of change. We are liberated from our bondage and awaken to find ourselves free, but without a clue about what that freedom means. We know how life works back in the prison, but we don't know how to live as citizens of God's Realm. We are confused and we need someone to explain what has happened to us and what we do now.

We are living in a foreign land. We don't know the customs and we don't know the language. So what do we do? If we were children, we would learn the new way of life and the new language simply by doing and speaking. No instruction would be needed because the way of life would form in us as we participated in it with others who already knew the culture. Adults, however, as fully formed humans, must make a connection between what we already know and the language we do not yet speak. This can be done through trial and error, in the manner of anthropologists learning the culture and language of an isolated tribe, or it can be done through a combination of instruction and participation. Instruction provides the translation; participation provides the sensual "allowing-in."

I became a unicycle rider by doing it through trial and error. It took a week to learn because I did not understand the principles of balance. Understanding the principles of balance would not have given me the skill, of course, but it would have provided connections to what I already knew and allowed me to use existing skills to help me ride. I could already ride a bicycle. I could already water ski. I could already balance on one foot. What I didn't know was how to use my existing balancing skills to learn an entirely new skill. There was no one to translate for me.

North Americans who are accustomed to their creature comforts tend to experience culture shock when they first enter a Third World country where few people speak their language. I remember my first exposure to Mexico in the late 1960s as a longhaired, very white teenager in bell-bottoms. I walked across the bridge into Nuevo Laredo with my blonde sister (who was wearing a skimpy sundress). To say we attracted attention is an understatement. We felt like aliens visiting another planet. People stared. Men hooted at my sister. We couldn't believe how different it was from suburban Tallahassee. Before they would allow our family to drive into the country, the border police forced me to have my hair cut by a barber who could (or would) only say "short or long" in English. I said long; my father said short. As we drove through towns and villages on our way to Mexico

City we heard, smelled, and observed many new things. There was meat hanging outside shops with flies buzzing around, women nursing children in public, goats bleating in the back of restaurants while we ate their roasted friends, and poverty like I had never seen.[21] Amid the shock, there was wonder, and I have been back to Mexico many times since. But that first trip was almost over before I was able to feel comfortable. How much more difficult would it have been without guidebooks in English, my mother's limited repertoire of Spanish phrases, and the occasional English-speaking Mexican?

Learning the way of Christ is not exactly like learning a new skill, a new language, or even a new culture. It is more like being transformed into a Mexican. A shocking exposure to Mexican culture is not enough. Understanding the language and customs is not enough. To be a Mexican, I have to feel like a Mexican, think Mexican thoughts, and generate new thoughts and behavior that are my own but have a Mexican flavor. I must be transformed into a Mexican. We must be transformed into Christians who incarnate the radical, ever-changing, ever-constant spirit of Christ in our own way.

The second stage of the transformational cycle deals with *understanding* our liberating new insight and how we begin to incorporate this new way of seeing into a new way of being. Like the ugly duckling who learns it is really a swan, we receive the stunning information that we are not who we have been pretending to be. The truth is sighted suddenly, but knowing that something is true doesn't transform our identity, nor does it show us how to live as swans or Mexicans. We must reinterpret what we had taken for granted in the light of our new insight. Only then can we begin to reconnect our past into a transformed present and see ourselves as whole again.

The primary function of adult religious education is interpretation and understanding. Obviously, however, interpretation is unnecessary if there

---

21. This description of my culture shock and my subsequent description of acculturation is not intended to demean Mexico or Mexicans. It is a Third World country, however, and thirty years ago it was a quite different place than it is today. It retained a very traditional character outside Mexico City and tourist areas. Women did not wear pants and tended to dress in dark colors. Driving and camping through Mexico from Nuevo Laredo to Mexico City, Veracruz, and back gave my family a much different perspective on the country than most tourists gain. Still, my culture shock had more to do with my insulated life in Tallahassee than with the nature of life in Mexico.

is no insight to unpack. Religious education without prior insight is a programmatic effort to form people who need to be transformed. It is pointless. It only adds more information to a system that does not know how to use it, and sees no reason to learn.

St. Peter Church in Cleveland channels the need for interpretation into a Rite of Christian Initiation for Adults (RCIA) class that combines several functions. The class, held on Tuesday evenings, lasts nine months and is for non-baptized adults who are interested in becoming part of the Christian community, but is open to anyone (including people who do not attend the church). Some people participate every year, and usually there are more repeaters than there are newcomers to the class. It is intended as an educational experience, yet as a subsystem of a larger transformational system, it creates a transformational flow of its own. The pastor provokes and evokes new *insight*, engages the group in a type of interpretation and struggle toward *understanding* not possible in worship, models *incarnation* through his person and the emerging (forming) community, and engages in spiritual *cultivation* through exercises of silence, contemplation and prayer. According to James White, RCIA "represents a recovery of the extended catechumate, which ritualizes the whole process of conversion, so the congregation shares in the individual's growth in faith."[22]

After one particularly evocative session, I talked to a man in his middle thirties who was taking the class for the second year. I was feeling rather stunned by the session because it challenged some of my own unexamined beliefs about the manner in which God inspired the writers of the Bible. I expressed dismay at having held rather childish beliefs for so long and my confusion over the loss. Brian smiled and said, "Yeah, it's great isn't it? He messes up my mind every week!" Even though the deconstruction of long-hardened beliefs in the class is painful, and was called "my crying time" by one female student, everyone experienced surges of growth as internal clogs were removed and our backed up systems started flowing through new channels.

INCARNATION

A religious education experience may include the entire transformational process, but it centers on interpretation and understanding—helping people

---

22. White, *Introduction to Christian Worship* , 205.

make sense of what they have discarded and what they are becoming. Using a transformational scheme somewhat similar to my own, Ross Keane suggests that "disorientation" is followed by "a search for meaning and peace [which includes] a search for identity, a seeking of personal integration."[23] But if the process is truly transformational, it cannot stop there. As Jack Mezirow notes, "transformation is never complete until action based upon the transformative insights has been taken."[24]

In order to continue the flow of the transformational system, the church provides channels for living out of a new understanding—for practicing the undeluded life. How does this happen? According to Avery Dulles, "faith cannot be transmitted in the cold atmosphere of the classroom or lecture hall. It is most successfully passed on by trusted masters in a network of interpersonal relations resembling the community life of Jesus and the Twelve."[25] This should not be surprising. Studies of human learning show that we learn best by observing someone doing something and emulating their behavior. We learn to reproduce *methods*—the actions others use to produce a desired result. Less intelligent primates learn to reproduce results by whatever method seems appropriate.[26] We create culture—patterns of behavior and ways of thinking—to get the job done. To learn how to be a Mexican, we must see how a real Mexican lives and experience that way of life ourselves.

The best way to learn a new language is to take one's intellectual understanding of what its words mean into a culture where the language is spoken. We emulate the speaking of those around us as we experience the speaking of the language ourselves. We try out what others are doing naturally. But in order to become Mexicans, rather than simply to learn to speak Spanish, we must go further. We must allow *Mexican-ness* to become part of us so that our actions are not mere imitation. We begin to incarnate what we were emulating so that what we are becoming is uniquely us, but

---

23. Ross Keane, *The Experience of Doubt and Associated Learning in Religious Men* (unpublished doctoral dissertation, University of Toronto, 1985). Referenced in Mezirow, *Transformative Dimensions of Adult Learning*, 177.

24. Mezirow, *Transformative Dimensions of Adult Learning*, 56.

25. Avery Dulles, *Models of the Church*, exp. ed. (Garden City, N.Y.: Doubleday/Image Books, 1974), 218.

26. Michael Tomasello, "Human See, Human Do," *Natural History* (September 1997): 47.

also obviously Christian. In other words, we do not become caricatures who ape actions by imitation. We become Christians with our own unique way of being Christian. Our incarnation takes the form of a vocation.

The process of transformation allows us to be liberated into a vocation where we can be truly ourselves. The way of Christ is not a way of bondage that requires us to act in a restricted and predefined manner. It is a way of liberation that enables us to live life as God intended. We reclaim our true vocation so we can begin to incarnate who we really are. According to Parker Palmer, "we are disabused of original giftedness in the first half of our lives. Then—if we are awake, aware, and able to admit our loss—we spend the second half trying to recover and reclaim the gift we once possessed."[27]

Learning the way of God's Realm involves a reversal of the way of the world. Rather than trying to live up (or down) to the expectations of others, we discover our vocation (our original giftedness), practice our craft, and bring our gifts to the community (family, church, world). We feast together on the gifts we all bring in celebration of God's surprising abundance. Learning this new way of being is difficult because we have been formed from childhood to follow a different path. We have been taught to make something of ourselves in order to merit rewards. The more we are able to get, the better we are. It is the cycle of conformity and consumption that keeps us striving and perpetually dissatisfied.

Bring Our Gifts —▶ **"To the Community"** —▶ **(We Feast)**

Rather than:

Extract from Others —▶ **"For Myself"** —▶ **(I Consume)**

The church provides a setting where a cycle of gift giving and feasting is modeled. We observe others doing it. We do it ourselves. We bring our gifts. We bless them. And then the gifts are returned to us transformed. They are more than the sum total of what was brought. The liturgy provides the model for life in God's Realm, and we experience it through our participation. By doing it ourselves—taking on the role of the doer—we

---

27. Parker J. Palmer, *Let Your Life Speak: Listening to the Voice of Vocation* (San Francisco: Jossey-Bass, 2000), 12.

allow the patterns into our bodies and thus into our being. Liturgy, more than any other experience in the church, exploits the natural way that we learn—the way that we build up rich patterns of meaning. According to Robert Marrone, "liturgy at its best is primarily sensual—it's about the body. It's about eating and drinking, hearing, seeing, smelling. It's the senses. . . . So why don't people understand? It's because they have not allowed it into their bodies. There has been no sensual 'allowing-in.'" In order to change the way people think and believe it is not enough to change what we tell them, "You have to change what people do . . . you work from the body to the abstract rather than working from the abstract to the body. [So] through the physical experience you will understand the spiritual experience."[28]

The church provides the practice field for an undeluded life of giftedness and a setting for feasting, but it is not the totality of God's reality. Our daily lives *are* God's reality and we are to live in that reality with the awareness of exactly who we are. We are gifted swans who love to feast. We are not deluded ducklings. We practice our craft in a world that wants us to conform (rather than to be who we are). That practice may seem unnatural, especially in the beginning. Yet the cycle of transformation leads to renewed minds, and to a reduced compulsion to conform. The way of Christ does not create a culture of conformity. It leads to liberation.

CULTIVATION

The process that began with liberation and continued through interpretation could end with incarnation. We could take our newly-grasped kernel of truth and let it enliven our actions throughout our lives. Such is the life of the zealot, the true believer who knows that they possess the truth. Most of us respect such persons, because they seem better than we are. They form our ideals but we don't think we will ever reach that plane of existence. Thank God we don't need to. We are not called to pursue truth like it is a deer we are chasing through the woods. We are called to open ourselves to truth and let it run through us.

In order to continue the process of transformation, we must stop and be still. When we stop, listen, and reflect we see what we were, what we have

---

28. Transcript of interview with Robert Marrone, pastor of St. Peter Church, Cleveland, Ohio, 1999.

become, and that we didn't do it ourselves. We didn't find the truth. It found us because we were forced to drop what we thought we knew. To paraphrase the words of Anthony de Mello, "awareness released reality to change us."[29] So what do we do now? We must drop our opinions again, including the new and better knowledge we have learned. But this time perhaps it is a little easier because we know that holding on to the truth is not the answer. To repeat the line that opened this chapter, "You have to remember to make it over again every day. . . . Otherwise it all goes to Hell."

What goes to Hell? All of it—our ideas about truth, our understanding of it, and the way we live it out. It all goes to Hell when we try to hold on to it and keep it from becoming something else. Essentially, we have to let it die. As de Mello says, "A fully alive person is one who is full of death. We're always dying to things. We're always shedding everything in order to be fully alive and to be resurrected at every moment."[30]

So what do we do? We shut up, be still, and let go—so that we will be empty enough to receive something new.

Cultivation means to prepare the ground for future growth—to become ready for new insights that will keep us from stagnating as the good people society wants us to be. It will involve contemplation, but not as a spiritual discipline that a good religious person must do. It includes practices that we should see as necessary for life, like eating and sleeping, because they allow us to do what all living things must do: change. When we clear the ground and allow the dust to settle, new things will be able to grow out of the richness of the soil we have helped prepare.

To use yet another non-religious example, I frequently receive insights on problems when I am in the bathtub. This happens so frequently when I am working on a major project that I sometimes keep a pen and paper near the tub in order to write down new ideas before I forget them. When I relax, slow down, and stop trying to figure things out, I open myself to a form of creativity that cannot be controlled through strictly rational processes. The truth emerges, as it will, from ingredients that are already available. For me, a nice hot bath is more than an indulgence; sometimes it is a religious practice.

---

29. Anthony de Mello, *Awareness: A de Mello Spirituality Conference in His Own Words* (New York: Doubleday/Image Books, 1990), 145. He also says, "The harder you try to change yourself, the worse it gets."

30. de Mello, *Awareness*, 151.

Through the many forms of contemplation, we open ourselves to the creative potential of God's reality. We drop our illusions—all of which we think are true—and we are suddenly in touch with reality again. Nature abhors a vacuum. When we empty ourselves, we will be filled.

DON'T GO THE OTHER WAY

When I presented the material contained in this chapter for the first time to a group of Unitarian Universalist ministers, two very helpful insights emerged. The first was to imagine the transformational cycle as a labyrinth walk. In the middle of it, things cook and stir through the energy of provocation and new insight. From that volatile place we move at our own pace through paths leading into the world.

The second insight was that the obverse of the transformational cycle forms a cycle of its own. It could be called a cycle of dependency and control. People must be *convinced* and then *trained* so they can be *used* for mission and ministry. And to keep them coming back, they must be *rewarded*. Guilt and shame also come into play as negative sanctions in order to keep the cycle going. If this cycle sounds familiar, it should. It is the process that most social institutions employ to control members' behaviors and to keep them inside. Churches are not exempt from becoming cycles of dependency, and in fact, may exemplify them.

A system is designed for the results it is getting. If you want different results, you have to redesign the system. A cycle of dependency produces controlling leaders and dependent people. Both groups remain insecure because followers never can be good enough and leaders never get the respect they deserve. We must redesign the system so it leads people into a life of giftedness rather than into a prison of unrealized ideals.

FORMING A TRANSFORMING COMMUNITY

We cannot save ourselves into a new way of seeing and being and it is unnecessary to try. Instead, we can enter a vessel that is running the cycle of transformation. It is the community that holds the language of the Kingdom and those who come in learn to echo the language that they hear.[31]

---

31. The term "catechumen" was used for persons who were being initiated into the church and means "to echo."

The purpose of the church is to be a vessel of transformation. It is the role of church leaders to help maintain the flow. But before they can do so, they must discern the current system. Is it a cycle of dependency and control or a cycle of transformation and incarnation? Resetting the system and restoring the flow is difficult. Usually it requires a series of shocks—provocations. Only then can the community begin the task of learning the new language of faith and practice being what they are becoming. And it will never "settle down." Accepting the normalcy of dissonance and change is part of the process.

Chapter ten

AN OPTIMISTIC ORIENTATION

"It was the best of times; it was the worst of times."[1] Doesn't Dickens's famous line describe the state of the church in the United States and Canada today? The mainline has been in decline since 1965, but we also are in an era of evangelical, charismatic, and Mormon growth. All across North America, small struggling congregations cannot afford a full-time minister (or pay a living wage to the minister that they have). Yet, on television and along interstate highways in major cities we see huge megachurches with five thousand, ten thousand, or even more members, complete with richly appointed sanctuaries and huge staffs. Many people are indifferent to religion, relegating God to an insignificant corner of their lives; others are deeply engaged in exploring their spirituality (inside the church and out).

In the midst of this confusing state of affairs, one thing is clear: the church is on its own. Churches are small businesses in a competitive economy. They must sink or swim based on their location, their ability to attract clients, and the size of their resource base. Churches have a product that requires participation to receive its benefit. Some people appreciate that product; others could care less. In North America, the former is about half the population. In England and Australia, no more than twenty-five or thirty percent of the population are churched in any meaningful sense.

Most unchurched or barely churched North Americans consider the church to be irrelevant, not very interesting, or both. They don't really need it except for baptisms, weddings, and funerals. Sundays are for resting and recreation. Going to church breaks up one's day to play. Everyone believes that you don't have to go to church in order to be a good Christian, so why put in the extra effort to attend? Unchurched Americans and Canadians are not antagonistic toward the church. They think the church is a good thing for society and particularly for children. Everyone ought to go more.

---

1. Charles Dickens, *A Tale of Two Cities* (1859).

In fact, they think they will go more often once they have kids (or once the kids they have get older). The number of "excused absences" each year now stands at fifty-one and includes every Sunday except Easter.

The reasons people attend church today are much more complicated than the reasons they do not. Most active churchgoers grew up in families that were very active in the church. Long exposure to anything helps form patterns of interest. Even when we profess to hate something we know only too well, there is a "home" quality to it that tends to draw us back. Still, we would not stay in the church unless we got something out of going. Benefits include a sense of belonging, meaning, control, comfort, and pleasure. People find friends in church and a sense of being part of a group, they discover purpose in life, they find moral guidelines and gain access to God's power, they feel God's love and the love of others, they are inspired by the music, challenged by the message of the minister, and experience the numinous. All of these things are considered products of the church and, like Mexican food, those that grew up on them consume them most regularly.

People come to the church because they are familiar with the language, culture, and religious tools that it provides, and they know how to use them to benefit their lives. People stay away from the church because they are unfamiliar with the language and culture and because they don't know what to do with its tools. Some people who grew up using religious tools drift away because they find secular tools more useful for their purposes. Other people who are unfamiliar with our language and tools, but need to do some religious work, make the effort to learn our tools and tongue. This latter population is rather small.

Since the culture treats the church as an outlet for religious goods, the obvious commercial reaction is to make our product better. We make our worship services more professional and powerful, we add new ministries to attract more people and keep them involved, and we even try to make God more responsive to our needs. In order to draw crowds, churches provide more God and more Mammon.

Mainline churches are uncomfortable with selling Christianity although they still do so in order to survive. They are the inheritors of a religious tradition that saw the secular state and institutionalized religion as equal partners in the control of the society and its citizens. They retain a benevolent, *noblesse oblige* quality that resists pandering to the public. It is not exactly "this is our product, take it or leave it," but it is close to "this is our product, take it because you need it."

Roman Catholic churches are the inheritors of an even older tradition—one that seeks to infuse religion into all aspects of life. In this totalizing tradition, the culture and the church are linked symbiotically. The approach was largely successful in creating a Catholic culture in Quebec and Mexico and a Catholic subculture in the rest of North America, but the barriers have broken down. Now Catholic churches must complete with the wider culture for their own constituency.

All churches seem out-of-touch and out-of-date except for evangelical megachurches. These imposing institutions are competing successfully in the North American religious marketplace. They are growing. Everyone else (for the most part) is declining, stagnant, weak, demoralized, small, and under-funded.

So what do we do? I suggest that we do not adopt the secularized success strategy of popular evangelicalism and try to market a better product. But this does not mean that we continue along the same track, doing worship in the same way, singing music written by dead European white men. We do not say to our constituency, this is what we offer: take it because you need it. Nor do we say, this is what we are offering, but how can we make it scratch where you itch?

We cannot go back and recreate a religious culture. The powers that be are not required to pay attention to the church. Also, the entertainment, self-help, educational, and life-management products of the church will never be as good as parallel products that are provided by secular society. We can't win that game, and we can't do much to fix the damage done by those who are winning. We need to get out of that game, stop dancing to society's secular tune, and recognize the business that we are in. Our business is to transform people, to wake them up; it is not to satisfy them with quality worship and engaging programs.

As with any system, our primary focus should be on the transformational processes that produce our product. If the processes are in place, the output will be good. And if the output is exceptional, it will be easy to attract the resources that will help us to produce even more. People are our products. Our product is not exciting worship, fun outings, craft classes, faith-based football, or professional programming.

People receive benefits and enjoyment from a transformational system, of course. The worship, preaching, education, ministry action, and opportunities for spiritual practice that make up the system cannot be objectively bad, boring, or old-fashioned. If they were, they would not contribute to the cycle of transformation. People would not be changed. Yet the primary benefit we get from the system is not solace, satisfaction, or personal enjoyment. Instead, the primary benefit we get is the capacity to deal with our problems. We create a transformational vessel with the capacity to create humans who joyfully participate in the creative unfolding of God's Realm—people who know how to live fully. What we gain is not comfort, although the support we feel from others and from our connection to God will make us feel better. What we gain is not control over our lives, although we tend to lose the sense that everything is out of control. What we gain primarily is the ability to see the world as God sees it and the invitation to live in that newly-realized world. When we stop trying to make everything turn out the way we think it should, and when we begin to use our giftedness to create a vocation, it is a lot harder to feel disappointed when things do not happen the way we expect. If all of life is sacred, nothing is profane. This is not fatalism, nor is it a passive acceptance of the status quo. Nor is it, I hope, the naive perspective of a pampered white American male. In order to recognize what we should do, we must be able to see the situation clearly rather than through egocentric interests or a controlling concern about what is right.

In this book, I have thrown in a lot of provoking statements, evoking images, and diagrams to channel a rethinking and rerouting process. The point is to begin a new thing—not to adopt a prepackaged one that I might provide. All churches are viable, living things that contain seeds of power. They can become transformational systems. What is required is radical change, but not all at once. Rather, we get the flow of the system going by making small, natural changes in our own actions after looking at what we are doing through the lens of purpose. We begin from where we are, as companies or corporations, charismatic-leaders-and-followers, and clubs or clans. Resolute action attracts response. People are drawn to it, and they bring their money and their time.

Once the sluggish stream begins to move, we augment the flow and let others help. We do not constrain its direction, however. We let it find its own channel. We trust in the incarnational principle for our church and, eventually, for our own lives as we participate in the transformational vessel and let ourselves be changed.

What the church becomes will be a surprise. We don't try to make it into a preconceived thing that we think all people need. We begin with worship and our personal interaction with core church members. We help reset the agenda and live out of the purpose that emerges. We do not radically alter the worship service, but we do begin to preach differently. We use the power of the gospel message to provoke a disconnection from unexamined assumptions. We evoke a different way of seeing and being. In time, we begin to work on other aspects of the worship service, replacing explanation with imagination, restoring story, parable, myth, and ritual. We sing songs that matter and create a seamless flow that people can step into without the need for instructions. We let people "become" the service and do it themselves through actions involving the whole body rather than just by mouthing words.

We augment the flow of the system through educational opportunities where people work out their faith from a new awareness. We augment the flow through ministry opportunities and the emergence of vocational identity. We augment the flow through spiritual practices. None of this comes in the form of requirements or obligations. Rather, the church forms a system through the actions of its parts (us). The church does what it does and evaluates what it does based on how its actions contribute to the transformational flow of the system. The most basic criteria is whether the thing is what it is supposed to be. Is it something else? If it is what it is supposed to be, then chances are it will do what it is supposed to do.

It is unlikely that the church as incarnational community will become huge. It will not be popular with everyone because it will irritate people who would rather sleep. Nevertheless, the incarnational community is fully alive and living things grow. People will be attracted in order to be changed. Changed people are grateful people and grateful people give.

I am both optimistic and pessimistic about the future. Wonderful things are likely, but there is a lot of decline and secularized ministry to be suffered through. I hope this book helps augment the optimistic options and does not impede their flow.

As I conclude this book, I am reminded of Ludwig Wittgenstein's last lines in the preface to his *Tractatus*. His feeling echo my own:

> If this work has a value it consists of two things. First that in it thoughts are expressed, and this value will be greater the better the thoughts are expressed. The more the nail has been hit on the head. Here I am conscious that I have fallen far short of the possible. Simply because my powers are insufficient to cope with the task. May others come and do it better.[2]

---

2. Ludwig Wittgenstein, *Tractatus Logico-Philosophicus* (Mineola, N.Y.: Dover, 1922), 28.

Index

Weber, Max, 61
what is our business?, Drucker
    question, 10, 25, 59, 131
White, James, 103n, 114n, 122
*Why Conservative Churches are
    Growing* (Kelly), 38
widgets, 50
Willow Creek Community
    Church, 2, 102
Wilson, Bryan, 8
Wittgenstein, Ludwig, 95, 133, 116,

117
worship: resources, 102; choreog-
    raphy of, 105, 107, 110; comfort
    function, 99n; contemporary,
    2–4, 14; evangelical, 103; main-
    line, 103

zero-sum game, 29

Other Books from The Pilgrim Press

THE BIG SMALL CHURCH BOOK
DAVID R. RAY

Over sixty percent of churches have fewer than seventy-five people in attendance each Sunday. *The Big Small Church Book* contains information on everything from practical business matters to spiritual development. Clergy and lay leaders of big churches can learn much here as well.

ISBN 0-8298-0936-8/Paper/256 pages/$15.95

LEGAL GUIDE FOR DAY TO DAY CHURCH MATTERS
CYNTHIA S. MAZUR AND RONALD K. BULLIS

This book belongs on every pastor's desk as the church is not exempt from the growing number of lawsuits filed each year. The authors are clergy as well as attorneys.

ISBN 0-8298-0990-2/Paper/148 pages/$6.95

FUTURING YOUR CHURCH
Finding Your Vision and Making It Work
GEORGE THOMPSON

Futuring Your Church allows church leaders to explore their congregation's heritage, its current context, and its theological bearings. George Thompson provides insights that enable church members to discern what God is currently calling the church to do in this time and place. It is a practical, helpful tool for futuring ministry.

ISBN 0-8298-1331-4/Paper/128 pages/$14.95

SO YOU ARE A CHURCH MEMBER
Revised and updated
ROBERT T. FAUTH

What does it mean to be a church member? What is the responsibility of a church member? These questions and more are addressed in this condensed handbook designed especially for new members of the United Church of Christ and other Protestant denominations.

ISBN 0-8298-1101-X/Paper/64 pages/$3.95

WONDERFUL WORSHIP IN SMALLER CHURCHES
David R. Ray

A valuable follow-up to the popular *The Big Small Church Book*, David Ray's latest work is specifically designed for pastors and lay leaders who are responsible for leading worship in small churches. Practical models of sermons, services, and guidelines for worship leaders are provided.

ISBN 0-8298-1400-0/Paper/192 pages/$19.95

YOU BELONG
A Handbook for Church Members, revised and updated
Allan H. Marheine

You Belong is a practical handbook for the new or veteran church member who wants to be more than a name on a membership roster. It provides useful insights for a local church member of any denomination.

ISBN 0-8298-1104-4/Paper/96 pages/$4.95

PATTERNS OF POLITY
Varieties of Church Governances
Edward LeRoy Long Jr.

All seminary students must take a polity class to prepare for ordination; this book offers an overview and a comparison of the major types of polity. *Patterns of Polity* provides a context for studying one's own polity with varied essays describing how each of the polities actually work.

ISBN 0-8298-1444-2/Paper/176 pages/ $16.00

To order these or any other books from
The Pilgrim Press or United Church Press, call or write to:

The Pilgrim Press/United Church Press
700 Prospect Ave E
Cleveland OH 44115-1100

Phone orders: 800.537.3394
Fax orders: 216.736.2270

Please include shipping charges of $4.50 for the first book and 75¢
for each additional book.

Or order from our Web sites at <www.pilgrimpress.com>
and <www.ucpress.com>.
Prices are subject to change without notice.